What is a Good Childhood?

Johannes Drerup • Gottfried Schweiger

What is a Good Childhood?

A Philosophical Approach

palgrave
macmillan

Johannes Drerup
Institute of General Education Science
and Vocational Education
TU Dortmund
Dortmund, Germany

Gottfried Schweiger
Center for Ethics and Poverty
Research
University of Salzburg
Salzburg, Austria

ISBN 978-3-031-74236-1 ISBN 978-3-031-74237-8 (eBook)
https://doi.org/10.1007/978-3-031-74237-8

This Palgrave Macmillan imprint is published by the registered company Springer Nature Switzerland AG.
The registered company address is: Gewerbestrasse 11, 6330 Cham, Switzerland

Acknowledgments

We would like to thank Monika Betzler, Nicolas Brando, Harry Brighouse, Doris Bühler-Niederberger, Julian Culp, Randall Curren, Doret de Ruyter, Melanie Ehren, Sebastian Engelmann, Franziska Felder, Michael Geiss, Anca Gheaus, Johannes Giesinger, Dorothee Gronostay, Michael Hand, Nina Hogrebe, Philip Kitcher, Meira Levinson, Veronika Magyar-Haass, Ruprecht Mattig, Roland Reichenbach, Anders Schinkel, Heinz-Elmar Tenorth, Werner Thole, Uwe Uhlendorff, Florian von Rosenberg, Lars Wicke, Lothar Wigger, Lynne Wolbert, and Miguel Zulaica y Mugica for discussions and helpful advice. Many thanks also go to the publisher of the German version of this book for granting us the rights for the translation (Reclam) and to Hannes Fricke-Sonnenschein for his careful and thoughtful proofreading of the German version. Special thanks are due to Douglas Yacek for the English translation and his many insightful comments on the philosophical argumentation.

Contents

About the Authors

Johannes Drerup is Professor of General Education Studies at TU Dortmund University and Guest Professor at the Free University of Amsterdam.

Gottfried Schweiger is a senior scientist at the Center for Ethics and Poverty Research at the University of Salzburg.

CHAPTER 1

Introduction

All children deserve a good childhood. Few would disagree with a claim of this nature. But what exactly makes for a good childhood? How do we know if we have experienced one? These questions are easily posed, but not so easily answered. They evoke a multitude of different and often conflicting associations. Everyone has had their own childhood, which they experienced as good or bad, or at least as better or worse in certain respects. When dealing with one's own childhood and with that of others, several different patterns of interpretation are invoked, some biographical, some sociocultural, and some historical. In these patterns of interpretation, very different ideas of a good (or not as good) childhood often come to bear. While some nostalgically indulge in memories of their own childhood as a kind of lost paradise, others see their childhood as a nightmare from which they are glad to have woken.

The great importance attributed to childhood in individual and collective self-interpretation is an expression of an incredibly powerful pedagogical insight: Childhood represents a special phase of life with its own value, the shaping of which in relationships and institutions often determines the course of a large part of later life. In everyday life, we talk quite naturally about how a person 'had a hard time in their childhood' or 'had a happy childhood.' We usually assume that we cannot understand the adult person if we do not understand their childhood, that is, if we do not understand how they have become who they are. We assume that

J. Drerup, G. Schweiger, *What is a Good Childhood?*,
https://doi.org/10.1007/978-3-031-74237-8_1

childhood is a phase of life that can be evaluated on the basis of evaluative criteria, a phase of life that can turn out better or worse. The topic of a good childhood is an existential problem that everyone deals with in one way or another, and we are likely to have strong opinions and judgments about it. In fact, discussions of childhood seem to attract strong normative judgments almost magnetically.

The question posed in this book—what is a good childhood?—may seem somewhat abstract at first. Yet it is not only a philosophical question but also a very concrete practical one. What makes up a good childhood is something we must all answer for ourselves, particularly in our dealings with children, in one way or another. In all areas of life in which people deal with children or think about children's lives—in schools, nurseries, or families, on the street or at the playground, at the doctor's surgery or in court—judgments are made about what is good or not good for children. It is therefore unsurprising that hardly any other topic can be debated so intensely and passionately, and that public and academic debates about the assessment of children's lives are often highly emotional. There are debates about children's nutrition, the establishment of daycare centers, and the building of playgrounds; the distribution of responsibilities for children between parents, communities, and the liberal state; the rights of children and parents; and the features that constitute a good childhood. All those involved in the public debate about children, which is rarely carried out together with children, generally claim to already know and be able to judge what is best for children. The normative criteria that govern how one evaluates one's own childhood and that of others are often implicitly assumed in these debates without consideration of what these criteria actually entail and how they ought to be weighted, justified, and applied. This regularly results in rather dogmatic assertions often lacking the necessary critical distance and systematic reflection on their plausibility and validity.

In everyday life, a good childhood is often understood to be a happy childhood. Children, as we are told in countless popular images and advertisements, should feel comfortable and secure, feel joy and have wonderful experiences. According to this widespread idea, a happy childhood is characterized by the subjective well-being of children, which is ensured above all by the fact that the relationship with parents and other close caregivers is characterized by love, care, harmony, and trust. This image, though not in itself objectionable, does not take into account the important distinction between a *happy* and a *good* childhood. Subjective well-being is an important aspect of a good childhood, but feeling subjectively happy, even for long periods of time, does not guarantee that one has had a good childhood. A child who is subjected to a thoroughly structured and coercive indoctrination regime, for example, can become accustomed to such conditions, and even experiences of violence, while being happy for long periods of time. If so, it would be implausible to call this a good childhood. The question of a good childhood should therefore not be reduced to the subjective experience of the child.

A good childhood, according to a *first* central thesis of this book, is a childhood in which a child is sufficiently provided with all the goods it needs to develop into an autonomous person. As we will show below, this also applies to younger children. These goods are not only of a material nature; the development of autonomy also requires many relational and educational goods of a nonmaterial nature—for example, love, care, respectful treatment, and basic education. We owe children a good childhood not only because these goods are beneficial to the children as children but also because this is likely to have an enormous impact on their future as adults (without necessarily determining this future). As much as we can hope that deficits in upbringing, education and socialization can be compensated for later in life, these deficits can severely and sometimes irreversibly impair the individual's ability to lead an autonomous and good life in the future. It may even undermine their very ability to experience happiness in the first place.

Of course, the importance of a good childhood for children is not limited to its impact on their future. Nor can it be reduced solely to the provision of goods relevant to developing personal autonomy. No good can be considered valuable *only* because it supports autonomy; it must also contribute in a real way to the individual's well-being. Consequently, a good childhood—now turning to a *second* thesis of the book—is a childhood in which a child is sufficiently provided with the goods it needs for its well-being. In addition to the development of autonomy, a child's well-being is the second central point of reference for developing a conception of a good childhood. Here, a distinction can be made between a subjective and an objective assessment of a child's well-being. This can be shown using the example of physical and mental health. It is intuitively plausible that health is an important element of a child's well-being and therefore also a component of a good childhood. A childhood can be considered better if a child is healthy. Health is not to be equated with feeling healthy, but can also be determined by objective physiological criteria. In the end, these criteria are more important than the child's subjective assessment. Children's well-being cannot be adequately determined on the basis of a single criterion either, but only along different core elements of a good childhood, each of which enacts central goods that are constitutive of children's well-being. These include so-called intrinsic goods of childhood (such as free and structured play), educational goods (e.g. basic education), and relational goods (e.g. love, care, and friendships).

This brief outline already shows that there are interactions and connections between the different core elements of a good childhood, between enabling personal autonomy and other goods, as well as between a good and a happy childhood. Much of what constitutes a happy childhood is also relevant to a good childhood. Child well-being and the development of the child into an autonomous person are also closely linked. Love and care are just as important for this as health and basic education. However, the different core elements of a good childhood are often in tension with each other, which sometimes manifests itself in conflict.

Children are people who only gradually develop into autonomous individuals, that is, gradually and with regard to different areas of life. At the same time, they have wishes, concerns, and projects that are important to them from a very early age, and they increasingly have the ability to articulate their importance to others. They can demonstrate and enact their will, which is often directed against the will of their parents and other caregivers. Dealing with the resulting conflicts is a central challenge of education in the family, in kindergarten, and at school. The question of what constitutes a good childhood is directly affected by such conflicts.

This addresses a *third* central thesis of this book: A good childhood closely depends on whether sufficient space is given to the child's will, wishes, concerns, and projects. We see this as an expression of appreciation for the child's developing autonomy and respect for the child as an individual person. Of course, a child's autonomy is not yet a mature and fully developed autonomy, and it goes without saying that a strong will cannot always be interpreted as an expression of developing autonomy. Children only gradually become autonomous individuals and are dependent upon supportive social and educational practices during their upbringing. Nevertheless, what we value and respect in mature, adult autonomy is already inherent in childhood autonomy. A good childhood is therefore a childhood in which the child is taken seriously as a person, along with his or her abilities, needs, and interests. This does not mean that a good childhood requires parents to hover around their children to meet their every whim and desire. But it does mean that we cease seeing children as appendages of their parents—that is, as deficient beings whose fate can be arbitrarily decided upon. In the context of a good childhood, a balance must always be struck between respect for children's autonomy and the need to restrict this autonomy for the sake of their well-being. The relationship between children's autonomy and vulnerability, between freedom and restriction, is different at every stage of childhood. While the protective function is of central importance for toddlers, the child's incipient autonomy must be taken into greater account in later phases and granted more freedom of expression. Such ethical considerations are of practical importance and unavoidable in educational contexts, where practical judgment and pedagogical tact are essential.

Just like adults, children are a heterogeneous group. Childhood is an enormously diverse and dynamic phase of life, which is why a concept of a good childhood must be sensitive to the differences between children at different stages of development. This is an important starting point and limitation of the scope of the following argument. In this book, we are concerned with the phase of life up to the onset of puberty. We consider this phase to constitute childhood proper. Sometimes adolescents are also referred to as children (e.g. according to the United Nations definition of a child, which takes the age of legal adulthood as the benchmark), but this does not seem to be a plausible starting point to us in the context of the question of a good childhood. The differences between children and adolescents are simply too great to accommodate within a theory of childhood; the adolescent phase of life poses unique tasks, challenges, and problems. Of course, the transition between childhood, puberty, and adolescence is fluid—that is, historically, socioculturally, and individually variable (see: Honig, 1999; Andresen, 2005)—but this does not mean that no distinction can be made between these two phases of life, nor that how we classify the two is arbitrary. 'Childhood' may be a social construct, but we cannot construct children howsoever we may please. Or, as the German philosopher of education Klaus Prange (2000, p. 236) has put it: Constructions don't cry and don't wet their diapers. Anyone who deals with real children will be able to confirm this pungent fact.

The concept of a good childhood that we advocate in this book claims universal validity. That is, our discussion of the goods involved in a 'good childhood' is to be understood as an ethical analysis of childhood as a universal human phenomenon, whose *normative scope of validity* is not limited to particular childhoods in some local contexts. While our analysis generally concentrates on the conditions of childhood in Western liberal democracies, this does not exclude the possibility that the basic core elements of a good childhood are relevant for all children and childhoods, even if they will need to be formulated and interpreted in a context-sensitive manner.

The answer to the question of a good childhood is of great educational, political, and social relevance—particularly, for the design of social and state institutions and the establishment of educational and intergenerational relationships. According to our argument, children have a moral right to a good childhood. They are wronged if their childhood is bad, assuming it could have been better, that is, if a certain minimum standard is not achieved and guaranteed. Many educational processes necessary for a good childhood naturally take place within the family. However, education and upbringing outside the family in kindergarten and school are undoubtedly of great importance for a good childhood. In other words, a good childhood is not a private project of the parents, even if the family is a central place for its achievement. A good childhood depends on social, economic, political, and cultural conditions. We have already mentioned elements of a good childhood that go beyond the family—for example, basic education or health—as they can hardly be realized in modern societies in families alone. Here, the question of a good childhood touches on political debates about entitlements to an adequate basic education for all children, the consequences of social segregation along socioeconomic disparities, and the problems of supporting children from socioeconomically underprivileged backgrounds, to name just a few. A good childhood is therefore based on a series of preconditions—a social infrastructure—without which the goods that are central to childhood cannot be realized. These include legal requirements for the legitimate treatment of children and an adequate material standard of living.

The social and institutional foundations of a good childhood means that a good childhood cannot be guaranteed by the parents alone. This raises the question of who is responsible for ensuring that children have a good childhood. In our view, the relationship between family and state must be considered and evaluated with respect to children's moral right to a good childhood. Parents, we argue, bear primary responsibility for their children; however, the state should support parents in this task and intervene if their ability to provide a good childhood for their children is seriously impaired.

This brings us to the final topic of this introduction. The question of what constitutes a good childhood can be discussed from the perspective of a variety of academic disciplines. However, we are convinced that the notion of a *good* childhood unavoidably invokes ethical and philosophical considerations. There are two reasons for this. The first reason is that normative criteria are needed to characterize a good childhood. Although these criteria may be intuitively obvious in some cases, they nevertheless require critical and systematic reflection. Why does it make a childhood better if children are given the space to make their own decisions and are not constantly controlled by others or trained to blind obedience? Is it possible to have a good childhood without cultivating autonomy-constitutive skills and habits? And why should basic education be valuable for a good childhood? Can children who leave elementary school as functional illiterates also be considered to have a good childhood?

In order to formulate answers to such questions, we have to deal with values and norms—in this case, the values of autonomy and education for children's lives. This is a task for the philosophy of childhood in general and the ethics of childhood in particular. At the same time, appropriate answers to these questions can only be generated in discussion with other academic disciplines, such as educational research, psychology, the social sciences and medicine, all of which can provide important insights into what makes a childhood good or bad in certain respects.

The book is divided into four main chapters. The second chapter—*Children and Childhoods*—deals with classic questions in the philosophy of childhood. What is a child and what distinguishes children from adults? What characterizes childhood as a phase of life and what are its special features? The second chapter not only provides answers to these questions, but should also reassure those readers who are skeptical that our central question—What is a good childhood?—can be adequately answered at all. Such skepticism is usually based on objections relating to the historical contingency of childhood, its changeability, normative relativity, milieu dependency, and cultural pluralism, as well as the constructed nature of childhood. In dealing with these quite justified objections, we clarify some of the theoretical premises of our argument. For example, a conception of a good childhood should take into account the historical changeability and social plurality of ideas about what constitutes a good childhood. However, this view does not imply an unbounded relativism, according to which it would ultimately be a matter of opinion whether one has had a sufficiently good or bad childhood. In contrast to radically constructivist theories of childhood, we propose an empirically informed anthropology of human childhood that recognizes the historical contingency and changeability of childhood conceptions without ignoring the diversity of childhoods in human communities. At the same time, we argue that many of the standard characteristics used to distinguish children from adults (e.g. autonomy, vulnerability, and rationality) allow fewer clear-cut boundaries to be drawn between children and adults than is often assumed in everyday life. This is linked to fundamental considerations regarding the moral and political status of children in liberal democracies. According to our position, the interests of children should be given the same moral and political weight as those of adults, which does not rule out the legitimacy of unequal treatment in certain areas of life.

In the third chapter—*Core Elements of a Good Childhood*—the theoretical foundations of a concept of a good childhood are developed and defended against objections. We are not concerned with determining what constitutes the best possible childhood but rather what constitutes a sufficiently good childhood. A sufficiently good childhood comprises the provision of fundamental goods of childhood. These goods are empirically and normatively intertwined in different ways, but they can be organized into five distinct classes: material goods, relational goods, educational goods, intrinsic goods, as well as personal autonomy. These goods include material provision and health, love and care, basic education, opportunities for free and creative development, and personal autonomy, which as a specific meta-good of childhood has a special role among these goods. Some of these goods are also important for adults, but in a different form. In this way, a good childhood envelopes two central normative dimensions in temporal terms. On the one hand, it is about children leading a good life *as* children. On the other hand, it is about preparing them for a good life as adults. Childhood is a formative phase that cannot be undone, just as a bad childhood remains a lifelong companion for many adults. This means that the goods relevant to a good childhood are specific to each phase of life.

A good childhood expresses a balance between autonomy and protection—beyond radical pedagogical restraint and strict surveillance and restriction of children's living environments. A central point of contention concerns the role and value of personal autonomy in a concept of a good childhood. Against some communitarian conceptions, we argue that that the facilitation of personal autonomy is constitutive of a good childhood and that childhoods shaped by systematic manipulation or even indoctrination cannot therefore be qualified as good. This position not only has far-reaching consequences for the way in which children should be treated (e.g. at home, at school) and the way in which the goods of childhood (e.g. care or education) should be realized. It also leads to subsequent conflicts with more traditionally oriented communities and parents, which are unavoidable in pluralistic societies.

The fourth chapter—*Children, Parents, and Families*—deals with the relationship between children and parents. Parents have a significant influence on the well-being of their children. However, it does not follow from biological or social parenthood that parents are particularly well equipped to care for their children or that they are capable of realizing the forms of relationship and ensure the background conditions necessary for a good childhood. The determination and distribution of parental rights and duties and their protection by the state must be justified on the basis of and oriented toward children's moral right to a good childhood. According to our argument, parents have a responsibility to offer their children a good childhood. This also requires them to give their children a sufficient degree of autonomy and opportunities for personal experience, even if this means putting their own values on the back burner. Our position is opposed to giving too much legal and moral weight to the interests of parents in relation to their children, as is the norm in the public and political debate. However, what parents can do to realize a good childhood for their children is often limited by external sociopolitical and socioeconomic factors, in particular by the material hardship and precarious circumstances in which they live. In these cases, parents are entitled to support in their role of caring for children.

In the fifth chapter—*Childhoods in the Liberal State*—we argue that *all* children have a moral right to a sufficiently good childhood. The state is responsible for creating the best possible conditions for children in society and an appropriate framework for their growth. In addition, it is particularly important to support those who have special needs and to help children whose parents are unable to provide sufficiently well for their children. The state cannot directly distribute or provide all of the goods that are important for a good childhood, for example love and recognition. But it can create the conditions that make it more likely that these goods will become a reality for children. Moreover, the state is responsible for protecting children where they are at risk. A good childhood is the robust moral standard against which the state should measure policies that affect children's lives. This position has far-reaching sociopolitical implications that affect all institutions that have a particular responsibility to ensure a good childhood in modern societies. We conclude with a brief conclusion that summarizes the findings of the argument and formulates several strategies aimed at improving the lives of children.

References

Andresen, S. (2005). *Einführung in die Jugendforschung*. Wissenschaftliche Buchgesellschaft.

Prange, K. (2000). *Plädoyer für Erziehung*. Schneider Verlag.

Honig, S. (1999). *Entwurf einer Theorie der Kindheit*. Suhrkamp.

CHAPTER 2

Children and Childhoods

The purpose of this book—to answer the question: What is a good childhood?—will to some seem overly ambitious and even attract skepticism. The aim of this chapter is to address some of the possible reasons for such skepticism and, if possible, to refute them. In doing so, we refer to several central debates in the philosophy of childhood and set out some of the fundamental normative and methodological starting points for our argument. Among the most important reasons why one might be skeptical of our book's mission are problems arising from the historical contingency, changeability, and normative relativity of childhood; its status as a social construction; and the normative character and status of childhood as a concept and a human phenomenon. We address each of these points in Sects. 2.1, 2.2, and 2.3, respectively. In working through these problems, we develop an ethical account of childhood that is sensitive to the unique tasks, possibilities, and limits of childhood. The account clarifies how to grapple with pluralism regarding how to shape a good childhood, what positions it takes up in public debates about children and childhood in a liberal democracy, and what justificatory premises we should proceed from to construct a normative theory of childhood (Sect. 2.4).

J. Drerup, G. Schweiger, *What is a Good Childhood?*,
https://doi.org/10.1007/978-3-031-74237-8_2

2.1 Histories of Childhood and the Problem of Progress

A good childhood—the very phrase might seem kitschy or sentimental. Worse, it may seem to suggest a glorification of childhood by adults who project their own culturally bound ideals onto children, a slogan destined for the docket of political rallies. Historical childhood research has shown how dramatically constructions of childhood can differ between historical periods, sociocultural milieus and living situations and also how diverse the attempts to delimit and demarcate human life phases into generational orders have been (such as early childhood, adolescence, etc.; see, for instance: Turmel, 2008; Winkler, 2017). The fact that we can even conceive of the idea of a 'good childhood' is by no means historically self-evident. That we can do so follows from specific socio-structural, socioeconomic, and sociocultural conditions that have produced childhood as a distinct phase of life in the form we know it today.

The intuitions that many people associate with a good childhood are all historically evolved and contingent (i.e. they could be different). Moreover, our intuitions about childhood are often rather recent and depend on social factors that we are hardly aware of, such as the reduction in child mortality, socioeconomic and political changes in family structures, and the relationship between public and private spaces. In light of the different ways in which childhood is organized as a social status and the associated practical treatment of children, one might ask whether the problem of a good childhood can be addressed at all. Given the variety of political, pedagogical, economic, and other interests that have been articulated and enforced with regard to children, does the question of a good childhood not inevitably lead to the reproduction of a time-bound naiveté? Will the project of defining a 'good childhood' illicitly declare a particular, historically contingent, and essentially 'Western' idea of childhood to be a hegemonic norm for all?

The assumption on which such objections are likely based is incorrect. The fact that certain ideas of childhood have developed historically and that every reconstruction of a good childhood has a double historical index (i.e. the object is subject to historical change and the reconstruction is historically situated; see Wulf, 2001) *does not mean* that the corresponding ideas and ideals that can be associated with a good childhood have no normative validity. Just because we know that people in the seventeenth century, for example, drew on different norms and values when thinking and talking about children than they do today, and just because we can assume that people will draw on other norms and values in a hundred years' time, this does not mean that the validity of the corresponding normative considerations is all relative, nor that they cannot be justified. Reconstructing the more or less contingent genesis of certain normative guiding principles (e.g. in certain parts of the world and under certain socioeconomic and cultural conditions) can help us to critically scrutinize them. This does not automatically disavow the validity of the associated normative claims, but can even reflexively reinforce our belief that these claims can be justified and can claim validity. Knowing that the emergence of the idea of childhood as a modern pedagogical conception[1] depended on certain sociopolitical measures (compulsory schooling, prohibition of child labor and the like) can also help us to evaluate these measures as a more or less desirable development overall. While the relevant research can enlighten us about the historical development and variability of normative notions of childhood and the social organization of childhood, it does not yet provide information about how corresponding developments and ideas *should* be evaluated. Even if we, for instance, want to reject overly romantic myths of a free and unencumbered childhood (see the critical analysis of Baader (2004)), images of childhood from the Romantic period can also be incorporated into a conception of a good childhood without their origin disqualifying them as *normative* guidelines (see the account of Gopnik (2016), which is based on empirical research on children and their capacities).

We should also recognize that historians' reconstructions of childhood are generally full of implicit, crypto-normative, or explicit value judgments about what constitutes a good or bad childhood. Such judgments are sometimes motivated by an implicit understanding of the current *Zeitgeist* and issue in a form of cultural criticism. From the perspective of historiography, such analyses may be criticized as anachronisms that project onto the past a current normative understanding of childhood as a decontextualized universal standard. From an ethical perspective, however, they can serve as important points of reference for ascertaining how current norms and values have developed historically and on which socio-structural and institutional conditions and processes of cultural change this has depended (such as changes in family relationships and forms of work). This can help,

[1] See for the distinction between a basic concept and different conceptions of childhood: Archard (2015).

then, to examine what can (and cannot) be learned from history or different histories of childhood for an analysis of a good childhood. After all, how can we reflect on a current ethical standpoint if we do not take note of the historical processes of change that have contributed to its formation? What are we supposed to learn from as historical beings if not from history?

A historically sensitive discussion of this topic will not make any claims to eternal legitimacy nor claim, for example, that today's childhoods are the 'best' in historical comparison. Rather, one can point out that corresponding judgments about progress and regress in dealing with children—as in the classic histories of decline and progress by DeMausse and Ariés—always presuppose assumptions and criteria about what constitutes a good childhood in certain respects. The systematic philosophical problems of explicating and clarifying the assumptions and criteria of a better or worse childhood, even in historical comparison, cannot simply be solved by referring to historical differences and transformations (which is often assumed as a foregone conclusion). From this point of view, the historical development of the object and the historical situatedness of the reconstruction do not imply any historically justified relativism on the order of, say, 'in the past this was true, today something else is true, and tomorrow something else will be true.' Rather, both forms of situatedness open up the possibility of a less naïve and more clearly contoured reflection on what one can and should imagine to be a good childhood, bearing in mind historical differences and past normative horizons of possibility. In other words, if one wants to answer the question of a good childhood appropriately, one must not only know whither the journey should lead, but also whence one comes historically.

The concept of a good childhood that we discuss in the next chapter can itself be understood as a normative interpretation of a change in social norms taking place in liberal democracies. This change can be interpreted not only as a historical learning process but also as an example of social and moral progress. This is because children are increasingly recognized to be individuals in their own right, instead of being regarded as mere objects or property; there is more genuine discussion with children today than perhaps ever before; their subjective emotional world and individuality are taken far more seriously than in other times; and attempts are made to understand children instead of merely forcing them into existing behavioral strictures, demanding blind obedience, or ignoring them altogether (Dornes, 2012). Traditional relationships of authority and violence have been and continue to be denounced and legally restricted; educational arrangements and practices for children have been rationalized and humanized (Berger & Fend, 2019; Pinker, 2011); and children's rights have been codified and institutionalized. The situation of children is the subject of constant public controversy, which often focuses on the particular vulnerability and well-being of children rather than their role as mere bearers of human capital. Children can also increasingly express their voices in public and stand up for their own interests or for those of others, and they can do so without this being always dismissed as mere childishness. Finally, the social fact that, at least in Western societies, children no longer have to toil in factories as they did in the nineteenth century and are therefore no longer integrated into the labor market at a young age is an incontrovertible success, as are other forms of relief from the burden of responsibility that characterize modern childhoods in some non-Western cultures.

Of course, these developments, which in our view represent objective moral progress overall, do not exclude the possibility that they are accompanied by negative side effects or consequences of an ambivalent nature for children (see, on this: Honneth et al., 2022), consequences that are worthy of critical attention. There may of course be a great need for further improvement, that is, for counteracting negative features and side effects of modern childhood(s) and for addressing the new challenges that our world presents young people. However, in order to be able to identify and address these needs, one must be able to employ well-founded normative criteria that indicate why childhood has become worse *in certain respects.*

Of course, it is easier to assert when progress and regression have occurred rather than to demonstrate systematically that a particular practice constitutes a real improvement from an ethical, political, and pedagogical perspective. For the purposes of our argument, it is sufficient at this point to name a few problems within what we call 'skeptical positions' on childhood progress—often found in certain power theoretic conceptions of childhood and in many programs of child liberation.

First of all, even the most radical skeptics of progress, if confronted with relevant historical documents, would not likely deny the obvious differences that characterize childhoods in modern liberal democracies as compared to other historical or national contexts, at least in certain respects. It is precisely in the normative reaction, for instance, to the pedagogy of violence (Rutschky, 1977), particularly in the context of National Socialism

(Tenorth, 2003), that ethical, political, and pedagogical value judgments are likely to be expressed. These judgments performatively, if not explicitly, question the thesis of nonexistent progress. Yet due to a global skepticism toward normative positions and debates, the skeptics prefer to hide behind the coolly distanced posture of the analyst of power or the spirit of the cultural commentator committed to critique. In these cases, one's normative sensitivities become crypto-normative judgments hidden behind implicitly moralistic descriptions of childhood, its status or its development.

However, researchers of childhood with power theoretic ambitions hardly ever seem to keep their normative judgments under wraps, as they ultimately want to make a decidedly critical statement about childhood. Sadly, this generally occurs without considering their own normative criticism to be in need of normative justification. After all, some theorists of childhood seem downright incapable of saying anything positive at all about contemporary forms of childhood, let alone accepting any notion of improvement or progress with regard to them. Indeed, they go so far as to claim that even the most obvious form of humanization in dealing with children (such as the abolition of corporal punishment) can actually be interpreted as a disguised and perfidious technology of power: If physical violence against children is outlawed, it is only because they can be better controlled and subjugated in other ways. If we try to take children seriously as subjects and give them scope for autonomy, this can only be interpreted as an internalized neoliberal mode of oppression and a form of socially induced self-coercion, which, they claim, must inevitably lead to depression in later life. Parents read books to their children, primarily for reasons of social distinction and as an investment in the human capital to be developed. Institutions are set up to try to guarantee children's health—this is but pure biopolitics that amounts to totalitarian control of family life and discriminates against minorities. Critics do not stop here; they claim the public school system should also be abolished, as it should be obvious that schools are nothing more than another pernicious disciplinary apparatus and an inequality (re-)producing enterprise, without which children in modern societies would surely be better off. In this rather gloomy world of theory and thought, there can be no progress in dealing with children.

Many such critiques can themselves be read as an expression of the so-called paradox of progress, since they can only be formulated on the basis of factual normative progress, to which they give expression in their allergic reaction to even the most trivial forms of injustice or exercise of power. In some cases, exaggerated and cynically negative worldviews seem to say more about those who propagate them than about social reality and the problems of real children. As important as the power factor is in dealing with children, using normatively charged metaphors or invoking the typical philosophical pantheon as received authorities (Foucault et al.) is not enough to justify the corresponding diagnoses of decline. One must also put forward *arguments* for one's own normative views and justify why and in what respect certain conditions concerning children are worthy of criticism. One must show that, although many children in Western societies seem to be doing quite well, this supposed progress should be classified as regression (Dornes, 2012). Instead of instrumentalizing children as projection surfaces for one's critique of modern societies and serving one's own prejudices on the basis of symptomatic misconceptions, it is important to name relevant power asymmetries between adults and children in their historical development and make a case for what a *legitimate way of dealing with these power asymmetries* might look like. Approaches to power theory, which are unable to distinguish between more or less desirable conditions and developments affecting children and instead seek to subsume these solely under the broad headings of power, domination, and violence, ultimately run the risk of not being able to normatively distinguish between obvious forms of mistreatment and legitimate pedagogical practices. Instead, the claim seems to be that one regime of power, domination, and violence simply replaces another; whether it is better or worse cannot be determined.

Such views do not seem plausible to us, partly because they amount to a conceptual and normative impoverishment of the debate on children and childhood. There is no question that power theoretic approaches have a certain analytical potential to reflect on the role of oppression and domination in historical and contemporary childhoods, to question traditional assumptions in public and academic discourses on children and childhood (e.g. on child development and the social functionalization of images of childhood), and also to examine naïve programs of progress for their dark sides (e.g. from a postcolonial perspective). However, these approaches themselves are usually accompanied by implicit ethical and political programs that they apply to children and childhoods without sufficient critical and methodological self-reflection. As such, they cannot justify their own claims to validity in a theoretically comprehensible manner.

The same applies to programs of child liberation in older conceptions of emancipatory pedagogy as well as more recent work done on the so-called topic of *childism* (see, for instance: Wall, 2022). In their critiques of contemporary childhood, both share a general tendency to ignore or deny progress in dealing with children. By advancing various narratives of decline, they tend toward the view that contemporary Western societies and their institutions should be interpreted primarily as complex apparatuses of oppression that are hardly compatible with a truly good, that is, above all 'free' childhood. From childhood histories, they conclude that any power imbalance between children and adults should be considered scandalous. The abolition or reduction of this imbalance is, according to these views, the primary criterion for identifying progress in dealing with children. Accordingly, they advocate freeing children from social power relations as early as possible and in all areas of life. Children have a singular interest in their own liberty, so they claim, which then miraculously conforms to the guiding principles of their decidedly anti-pedagogical and anti-paternalistic program.

From this perspective, a good childhood would be above all a childhood in which children participate in common life as much and as actively and freely as possible, always and everywhere, and are otherwise spared any kind of paternalism by adults. A good childhood would therefore be a childhood without pedagogical and educational arrangements, a childhood in which the social status of 'childhood,' which is itself interpreted primarily as a repressive construction, has itself been abolished. Everything will be fine, so the argument goes, if we just let the children do it. In the end, they can help us save the world, because with their children's eyes they are capable of very special insights that adults lack in their worldview, a worldview that has been corrupted by their own oppressive educational experiences.

Within the framework of such doctrines, children function as a kind of substitute proletariat that only needs to shake off their chains of false consciousness and oppression in order to finally be free to reform the (adult) world for the better. The fact that this narrative itself amounts to an instrumentalization of children for a particular political agenda, and one that is by no means new, generally goes unnoticed by the politically ambitious protagonists of child liberation. In their more recent variants, liberationists adopt views from the 1970s almost one-to-one without taking note of the corresponding debates that have taken place in recent decades.

If the history of pedagogical and educational debates is not taken into account, then nothing can be learned from this history. Instead, the same old formulas and slogans are used (children are unique, children are our everything, look at the world through the child's eyes, etc.), and once again we maneuver ourselves into philosophical dead ends that we thought had long been overcome.

Apart from the obvious theoretical deficits and the kitschy, one-sided and unimaginative nature of these positions, it cannot be denied that child liberationists provide important insights, such as the prevalence of adult-centered perspectives, adultist prejudices, or unconsciously reproduced educational pathologies handed down over generations (see the more instructive and interesting notion of childism developed by Young-Bruehl (2012)). In the end, however, liberationist perspectives are hardly suitable for adequately discussing and answering the questions and problems that they themselves raise. Like approaches based on power theory, liberationists tend toward moralizing and overly general condemnations of children and childhoods (which are then constructed per se as a marginalized group that is discriminated against on the basis of its age).[2] The liberationist position can and should be taken note of in discussing the meaning of a good childhood, but it is unlikely to be of much help in providing a historically informed clarification of the ethical criteria of a good childhood or the conditions needed to realize it in practice.

In short, the fact remains that the question of progress and the question of the core elements of a good childhood cannot be answered independently of each other, as neither progress nor regression can be identified as such if one does not have criteria that could justify such normative judgments. The skeptical positions described above and the narratives of decline that often accompany them do not provide such a justification, even if it can be conceded that they tend to appear in a culturally critical style and are not exactly sparing with normative judgements. Rather, our claim is that we can learn from the history of childhood, particularly from a normative perspective. We can do so *ex negativo*, for example, by historically contextualizing relations of power and violence and viewing them from a contemporary perspective (such as the history of child abuse or poverty or the various failed social experiments of collective education; see, von Rosenberg, 2022). And we can do so positively by examining

[2] For a discussion on the moral relevance of 'childhood' as a social category, see also Brando (2023).

what may have improved in the treatment of children over the last few centuries. Of course, it is then necessary to demonstrate that the results of this examination constitutes an improvement. It is this specifically ethical step in our chain of reasoning, so often missing in prior analyses of childhood, that can iteratively (and not just subsequently) inform the historical analysis. Thus, in both negative and positive ways, the history of childhood can help us to broaden our imaginative and practical horizons, preventing us from committing ourselves to the misguided presentist view that there can be no viable alternatives to how childhoods are shaped in modern societies today.

2.2 Childhood as a Social Construction

Another problem that an ethics of childhood should address is the question of the constructed nature of children and childhood. According to a central guiding assumption of social science research concerning childhood, 'childhood' and 'children' in different times and social contexts is a question of construction. According to this thesis—put forward with varying degrees of radicalism—childhood, and thus also the difference between children and adults, is first and foremost a social construction. As such, childhood is not a mere biological fact; it is produced discursively within a framework of practices and institutions that has always been socially and culturally shaped. Children are not simply there; they are made into what they appear to us to be. One's understanding of childhood always depends on the prevailing understanding of what actually constitutes the status of an adult, and vice versa. Children, so the argument goes, have historically served and still serve today as critical projection surfaces through which adults articulate and demarcate themselves from nonadults. While the latter can and want to be considered mature and rational, children are ascribed the role of immature and irrational beings, a deficit attribution that is also suitable for justifying different pedagogical and political power relations toward children as a special social group that requires special treatment.

The strength of the social construction thesis lies in the fact that it allows us to question and deconstruct cultural assumptions about the normality and ontology of our own conceptions of children and childhood (see, on this from a posthumanist perspective: Malone et al., 2020). This applies both to the scientific understanding of childhood and to public speech about children, in which it becomes obvious that children and childhood can be construed in very different ways. If this is the case, then it is possible to think and talk about children and childhood differently, perhaps even completely differently, and that the relationship between children and adults could be organized in unprecedented ways. Instead of seeing children as deficient, still unfinished adults and as passive recipients of educational interventions, the social construction thesis urges us to see children as active and capable actors who construct and participate in their own world. A deficit construction of childhood is thus replaced by a positive construction of children and childhood. This positive reinterpretation is often flanked by implicit assumptions concerning performative effects of differing practices of social construction, which assume that if we construct children differently, we will also treat them differently, which in turn leads to them act and develop in a different way.

And this is where the problems begin. For in many cases, the social construction thesis seems to take on several functions in the academic debate which are not always adequately distinguished from one another. It often remains unclear whether the social construction thesis is primarily part of a *descriptive-analytical* research program, according to which childhood is to be understood primarily as a culturally and historically variable category and social phenomenon, or a decidedly *normative* program, according to which it is *ethically and politically necessary* to regard childhood as a construction, a construction that could also be different and should ideally be replaced by other and more legitimate constructions.

The social construction thesis thus seems to be repeatedly underpinned by hopes of emancipation that emphasize the contingency and changeability of our ideas and practices. Children and childhood can be constructed and understood not only *differently* but also *better* than we do now. Is and ought—that is, the domains of theory-based empirical research and the ethics of childhood—thus regularly merge into one another. Unfortunately, such morally ambitious childhood researchers rarely make it explicit that they are moving on decidedly ethical terrain when they demand that children should finally be taken seriously as autonomous agents capable of coordinated action. This guiding principle of much childhood research is then sometimes itself criticized as an essentialist, Eurocentric, and Western construct (for example: Betz & Eßer, 2016) that ignores the fundamental dependency and vulnerability of children, often without engaging in the ethical question of whether it might not be justifiable as a normative goal beyond the relevant research methodological problems. In some cases, then the normative desiderata and expectations packaged in the social construction thesis remain without theoretical or empirical confirmation, particularly when children patently do not behave in accordance with the constructions ascribed to them, but rather in accordance with other political and pedagogical ideas and guidelines (Bühler-Niederberger, 2020). At this point, it becomes completely unclear what was actually meant by the social construction thesis, whether as a normative, perhaps even universalist proposal, or a purely descriptive thesis about how children are really to be understood.

As important as the insight into the social construction of children and childhood may be, this thesis is only convincing to a limited extent, especially in its radical constructivist guise. After all, neither children nor adults are mere moldable clay that can be constructed at will. The anthropology of radical malleability implicit in radical constructivism is full of troubling political implications and the potential for collateral damage (think of the 'new men' that were to be made out of children in historical attempts at mass education). This is another reason to be suspicious of constructivist understandings of childhood. In making such radical claims about the malleability of children and childhood, constructivist childhood researchers may have given politicians and other actors too much leeway to develop policies that ignore the real needs of children (Sidorenko, 2015).

Nevertheless, there are good reasons why one would prefer to limit oneself to talking about 'constructions of the child' instead of their supposedly 'innate nature.' Studies in the history of education and science show how variable and time-dependent anthropological assumptions have been within the framework of scientific disciplines (Baader, 2015). Contemporary discussions of pedagogical anthropology also point to the variety of different anthropological interpretations of children, all of which can be debated (Zirfas, 2021). There seems to be much to be said for a purely negative, historical anthropology, which does not claim to know what really constitutes the nature of the human child, but only about how this nature has been historically constructed in different variations. The assumption is that we cannot, and should not, fix human nature in essentialist terms, as such a definition would be ethically, politically and pedagogically questionable. Skepticism about essentialism concerning the human nature of children thus tends to go along with a normative condemnation of essentialism. In more radical versions, such an anti-essentialism then may imply that also scientifically approved anthropological assumptions about the objective nature of children and their development not only cannot exist (because they are merely time bound sociopolitical constructions) but also ***should*** not be taken into account.

It is rarely taken into account that such impossibility theses are themselves based on controversial anthropological assumptions, be it the abovementioned radical malleability of human beings, their ***perfectibilité*** (e.g. understood as the ability to develop human abilities), or, in a more teleological sense, their capacity or even destiny for self-determination. It is also rarely made explicit that these principles of anthropological criticism are themselves based on a strong normative impetus to avoid making anthropological assumptions about children for ***pedagogical*** and ***political*** reasons and not reasons based on ***empirical*** research on children. This critical abstinence is justified in part, for example, if one recalls how the tripartite school system in Germany was legitimated by reference to a supposed 'talent pyramid' among human beings, in which children were assigned to different types of school according to supposedly naturally distributed talents in the population.

However, despite this justified anthropological skepticism, it remains unclear whether its philosophical claims are really plausible beyond the rejection of essentialism. Even if we can relegate the essentialist construction of a child's nature to the dustbin of pedagogical and political history, and even if research into the history of science shows that anthropologically based developmental psychology operates with questionable, timebound premises, this does not mean that we cannot make empirically informed statements about the nature of children at all.

To give a simple, perhaps trivial example: If you take an infant and shake it violently, this will have starkly negative effects on the child (whiplash and the like), regardless of what culture it calls home. Whether we construct the infant as a competent being that constructs its own world also does not make a difference. If infants are not cared for and are instead left to vegetate alone in their beds for weeks on end, they wither away, lose weight, and are very likely to suffer psychophysical trauma (for historical cases as well as relevant empirical research, see von Rosenberg, 2022; Dornes, 2014). This also applies if they are exposed to constant psychological and physical violence. Or, to use another example: It is certainly important to remain skeptical concerning anthropological constructions of ***normal*** psychological and physical development of children. Nevertheless, it remains obvious, to refer to an extreme case, that if a child of eight years has lost all her teeth due to bad hygiene and nutrition, this certainly should neither be qualified as 'normal' age-appropriate nor as good development. These are all objective, anthropological facts that characterize human children, objective in the sense that we cannot construct them away as we please. Children are not only children because we treat and construct them as children; after all, they do not suddenly become adults when we start to interpret them in a way that is no longer age-appropriate. Even then, contrary to the naïve, almost magical assumptions of radical constructivists, children remain children. Children, especially infants and toddlers, *are* in reality more vulnerable in certain respects than adolescents and adults, objectively and independently of any constructions.

Even if the specific abilities and vulnerabilities of children are therefore always shaped by social structures, this does not change the fact that they are anchored in objective and universal anthropological differences between children and adults and do not merely represent products of attribution and production in social practices and discourses. An ethics of childhood can and should be sensitive to these differences. These defining features of children cannot be changed at will and demand to be dealt with differently depending on the context, not least by taking into account the results of various human sciences concerning children. This in no way means that scientific findings about children should be blindly accepted. Nor does it mean that they cannot be revised and require no further normative classification. Rather, an empirically informed anthropology of childhood has the task of examining their plausibility and critically scrutinizing the normative assumptions and constructions concerning children. Repeatedly using the essentialist hammer against empirical research is just as insufficient as generalized references to the constructed character of childhood. For example, older developmental psychological research has been criticized for relying on a deficit conception of childhood (Matthews, 2009), and in more recent versions, a lack of reflection about the history of romantic images of childhood can be detected (see: Gopnik, 2009). This does not mean, however, that developmental psychology cannot provide us with orientation on the anthropological characteristics of child development (see, for instance: Dornes, 2014; Gopnik, 2016; Tomasello, 2020). But if this is true, what exactly follows for an ethics of childhood?

Attempts to derive normative criteria *directly* from anthropological assumptions are doomed to fail, since such understandings of human nature always include normative assumptions that are themselves in need of justification. This does not mean that anthropological premises can be dispensed with in the context of an ethics of childhood. Nor does it imply that anthropological assumptions cannot provide *clues* as to what is normatively relevant for determining what a good life for children is, or what can be done with them in good conscience. The results of empirical research on children and childhood (e.g. from medicine, educational science, childhood research or psychology) can help us understand which conditions and relationships are conducive to the appropriate and successful development of children. What we consider to be 'appropriate' in this context itself requires its own normative justification, which cannot be derived from the results of empirical research and corresponding anthropological premises. By nature, children are not initially destined for anything, not even self-determination. However, they naturally bring certain biological preconditions into the world that must be taken into account. These biological preconditions are always culturally and socially shaped. Nature and nurture are therefore always already intertwined in processes of education and upbringing (Giesinger, 2009).

The results from childhood research presented here can thus sensitize us to the different ways in which children and childhoods have been discussed and the anthropological definitions and omissions that go hand in hand with these discussions. However, this must be separated from the ethical and political question of how such constructions, and the projections on which they are often based, are to be evaluated, both in terms of their empirical and normative plausibility. For it obviously makes a practical difference how we construct children and what premises we start from. Think, for example, of the practice of bandaging children from toe to neck because it was believed that this would protect them from danger and at the same time ensure that they would grow sufficiently 'straight.' People were convinced of the correctness of this practice, which of course does not mean that it was correct, not least because the underlying empirical premises are incorrect according to current knowledge. This means that constructions of childhood and anthropologies of childhood can be critically scrutinized in the light of scientific findings, findings which, although they have a historical origin and are fallible, can be examined for their appropriateness. In the context of an ethics of childhood, an empirically informed anthropology has a pragmatic corrective and orientation function that can provide information about the characteristic anthropological conditions that ethical reflection must reckon with, whether they conform to certain constructions of childhood or not. On a positive note, the debate about the constructed nature of childhoods also shows that there is a great deal of scope for shaping the reality of a good childhood, a reality whose proper evaluation cannot be derived merely from anthropological premises.

2.3 Childhood as a Moral Status

Childhood is a thick concept, that is, a concept that encompasses both descriptive and normative elements (Betzler, 2022). The former includes anthropological and psychological assumptions about childhood, while the latter, at least in modern conceptions of childhood, includes the normative assumption that children have a specific moral status. From this status, we can infer that we have certain obligations toward children that we do not have in the same way toward adults.

With regard to questions concerning the *descriptive* elements of childhood, we should first consider anthropological factors following from the previous section. These include the need for education, the ability to learn and develop, relative dependency or lack of independence, vulnerability, and a certain power or maturity gap which manifests itself in the generational difference between children and adults. Accompanying these characteristics are the differences in knowledge and experience between children and adults, as well as the factual deficits that children exhibit in certain respects (including rationality and self-reflection skills) compared to most adults. In our opinion, it is perfectly legitimate to speak of deficits here, as this does not imply that children do not have other relevant abilities that can be valued (openness, curiosity, imagination, and the like), nor that describing children this way necessarily labels them as deficient *tout court*. The tendency to deny these anthropological facts even on a descriptive level is itself generally based on normative conceptions of childhood; it also ignores the fact that without recourse to these facts, we inevitably run into problems concerning the justification of our special normative obligations toward children (see below). We therefore neither commit ourselves to traditional deficit conceptions (children as deficient beings and still incomplete adults) nor to one-sided romantic conceptions of childhood (children as little scientists, philosophers, and potential saviors of the world), but only name some of the most important anthropologically anchored, universal differentiating features of childhood. These are characterized by the fact that certain cognitive, emotional, social, and physical abilities are only gradually and typically less developed in children, while the corresponding processes can of course vary greatly depending on the individual and social environment. Despite the many other differences between children (e.g. along the categories of age, class, gender, race, disability, etc.; see, for instance: Felder, 2022), it is also perfectly justified in this context to make generalizations and speak of children in general, at least if it is taken into account that neither the relevant differences nor the similarities between children are ignored.

We have already seen that dividing the lifespan into phases varies culturally and historically, just as the anthropological circumstances mentioned above also differ depending on the life phase. We relate the considerations that follow to the period before the onset of puberty (around the age of 8–12 depending on gender and individual circumstances) and therefore limit childhood to the period before adolescence (i.e. the onset of puberty and the pubescent stage). We take this approach for pragmatic and substantive reasons. Pragmatic because it limits the validity claims of our argument, the extension of which to other phases of life would have to take into account a number of other conceptual and practical problems; substantive because these life-stage-specific problems are accompanied by unique challenges (e.g. with regard to the justification of pedagogical paternalism) and are best addressed apart from theories and models of childhood (Betzler, 2021). Aside from this, one could also have used a particular point in time (e.g. the legal age of adulthood) as a demarcation criterion rather than puberty, since the latter is biologically and culturally variable. This may have some advantages, but we feel our approach is more anthropologically sensitive than a legalistic approach, even if in doing so, we cannot completely avoid a touch of the arbitrary.

With regard to questions concerning the *normative* elements of the concept of childhood, we assume that the aforementioned, anthropologically anchored differences between adults and children are suitable not only for distinguishing the moral status of childhood from the moral status of adulthood but also for justifying making such a distinction in the first place. Demarcations of this kind always come with difficulties, and we follow Johannes Giesinger's proposal in conceptualizing and dealing with the relevant issues (2019). On the one hand, the standard liberal view assumes that personal autonomy is a central criterion for distinguishing between children and adults, since paternalism toward sufficiently autonomous persons is considered illegitimate. Autonomy is then usually determined via threshold concepts that indicate when a person has sufficient abilities and competencies and is able to guide their own actions by means of authentic decision-making. Conditions for authenticity and competence must be defined at a very low threshold, since otherwise paternalism toward many adults who do not reach this threshold could be justified (e.g. minimal procedural rationality as the ability to absorb information and process it appropriately). At the same time, one cannot deny children at least minimal forms of autonomy, which then calls into question the legitimacy of educational and pedagogical paternalism. In pedagogical contexts, more ambitious educational aims will ultimately be pursued (such as autonomy qua critical self-reflection), but these are unlikely to be suitable as a generalized standard for the status of an autonomous person, as large sections of the adult population are unlikely to achieve it. So what normative standard should we use to determine the moral status of children as opposed to adults? And can it be legitimate to treat children and adults with similar abilities unequally?

One way of dealing with this problem is to use legal age requirements that simply lump all actors together, regardless of what skills they actually have. However, referring to such more or less arbitrary conventions does little to provide an ethical justification for the appropriate and legitimate treatment of children until they reach the appropriate age, given the differences in competence and development mentioned above. Another possibility is the introduction of individual autonomy tests, which would allow some sufficiently competent children to gain rights in certain domains that are otherwise reserved for adults (e.g. the right to vote). Not all children would then become adults or be considered adults at the same age. Such a sweeping change would almost certainly be associated with some collateral social damage (such as hierarchies and inequalities that develop between groups of children, often reflecting their socioeconomic background), not to mention significant societal expense.

Alternatively, the dilemma could also be resolved unilaterally, in the sense that one simply accepts that paternalism toward adults can also be justified. Or, based on a minimalist conception of autonomy, one could also argue that all children—regardless of their age—who are sufficiently autonomous in the relevant sense must be granted full autonomy rights. While in the first case adults might have to be treated 'like children,' in the latter case children would have to be treated 'like adults.' Both are likely to have questionable social consequences, especially for children who reach the minimum standard of autonomy. For they would, *ex hypothesi*, no longer be educated at the public's expense, and the usual moral duties toward these young adults and our responsibilities to them could no longer be justified. Similarly, the specific institutions and arrangements set up for them would also lose their normative justification.

Giesinger's resolution of this dilemma, which we consider plausible, therefore considers childhood and adulthood as having different moral statuses. The determination of this status is partially based on the criteria mentioned in the standard liberal view (autonomy-constitutive capacities and anthropologically anchored differences between children and adults). However, for Giesinger, these are not sufficient in themselves to justify unequal treatment between children and adults, nor do they allow a precise temporal and practical determination of the transition to adult status. According to Giesinger, a moral status can be understood as a bundle of entitlements and obligations that are attributed to agents within the framework of social practices and institutionalized structures. The transition from childhood to adult status, the timing of which is always to some extent arbitrary and dependent on social conventions, is accompanied by the attribution and acquisition of not only various rights (such as autonomy and participation rights) but also new obligations (such as paying taxes and working). Giesinger thus draws attention to an extremely important point that is insufficiently considered in some prior treatments of childhood, especially by child liberationists but also by some childhood researchers and historians. Instead of focusing primarily on the restrictions associated with childhood status, Giesinger highlights the many advantages and privileges associated with being a child in modern Western societies as a central aspect of an ethics of childhood. These include, for example, the relief from duties and responsibilities, the support and protection that children ideally receive from adults, and the extended time and social space that is granted to simply 'be a child'—progressively learning about the world and gradually preparing oneself for adult life.[3]

The modern idea of a protected and preparatory space relieved of responsibilities and duties in childhood therefore does not have to be interpreted as the incapacitation and exclusion of children, as illegitimate infantilization, or as a 'social pathology.' It can and should also be understood as a cultural achievement, as moral progress, which comes with the

[3] See also: Anderson & Claassen (2012). On the historical emergence, development, and implementation of corresponding ideas of a pedagogical moratorium in the Enlightenment and the associated controversies, see Zinnecker (2000); see also Andresen (2005). It should be taken into account that such ideas have often been used to justify questionable perspectives and hierarchies (such as gender hierarchies). Thus, the ambivalences, generational orders, and assumptions about children and their well-being in different life situations associated with them can be critically discussed from a historical and systematic perspective: Eßer (2014).

realization that childhood is a phase of life with its own value. Of course, one should not ignore the ambivalence that can be associated with this status (e.g. protection usually also means control). The protection and control that occurs in childhood, for example, could also be defined and organized differently than it is now, and the legitimacy of current institutional and social requirements surrounding children's rights is of course debatable (e.g. with regard to the right to vote). This is also true because the reshaping of childhood or a transformation of status would also be accompanied by certain performative effects. For example, if we treat children like adults at an earlier age and delegate responsibility to them, they will to some extent develop a greater sense of responsibility and be able to act responsibly in certain domains. There is a certain amount of room to maneuver here.

Advocates of child liberation who resolve this dilemma differently must therefore take into account the potential disadvantages for children that would be associated with a more or less radical shortening of childhood if they were to be released into adult status earlier, together with their specific vulnerabilities, their lack of experience, and their less-developed abilities. Ultimately, we should expect that this course of action would lead to new forms of inequality between children declared to be adults and real adults. In fact, the latter may no longer feel responsible to the former, as they would no longer be dealing with children. Whether it is actually in the interests of children to impose upon them the practical demands of personal autonomy and political responsibility is therefore doubtful. For these reasons, we agree with Giesinger that we should treat even those younger or older children who meet the requirements of minimalist conceptions of autonomy as children and to orient their upbringing toward more demanding conceptions of autonomy and other goods.

Such unequal treatment does not amount to a denial of children as social agents or a denigration of their interests in favor of adults. On the contrary, children, like adults, are human beings whose interests should be given equal weight from a moral and political perspective and should not be ignored. However, this *does not mean* that the morally relevant differences associated with their status as children should also be ignored and that they can and should be treated as adults. Rather, respecting them as persons also means recognizing their special living conditions, which include the fact that they must first be enabled to gradually develop a reflective attitude toward themselves and the world. At the same time, the aforementioned advantages of childhood status are linked back to assumptions about a good childhood, as this status can only be considered good for children if a sufficiently good childhood is guaranteed for them.

2.4 Childhoods in Pluralistic Societies: Justificatory Issues

We would like to begin this section with some caveats: Philosophers, and especially those who discuss ethical issues, sometimes speak as if they were clerics who bring truth to the people from the pulpit, 'from an ethical perspective.' However, philosophers are not clerics, nor do they have the role of preachers or saviors. In this book, we also do not offer advice in terms of a practical self-help book—that's for those who feel called to do so—nor do we claim that, on the basis of a conception of a good childhood, all possible problems relating to children can be resolved by simply applying general norms to individual real-world cases without further need of reflection. This would be naïve not only because application problems entail their own complex follow-up questions (from a lack of or disputed knowledge to unintended side effects) but also because, within the framework of liberal democracies, we have to live with the fact that even well-founded and justified ethical concepts can be politically enforced only through democratic procedures.

The aim of this book is to clarify what is meant by a sufficiently good childhood. In order to realize this goal, we will need to reconstruct and critically examine normative assumptions and intuitions about childhood, an endeavor which can be linked to the project of developing an ethical conception of a good childhood. When adults talk about children and childhood, they often face the suspicion that their claims are inevitably self-interested, since adults advance notions of childhood that often confirm their own experiences and prejudices. This psychologizing interpretation, which can be found in the debate in sometimes stronger and sometimes weaker forms, points to the risks of idiosyncratic, subjectivist theories of childhood. We will try to avoid this problem by looking at the philosophical and scientific debate on a good childhood. Of course, the conceptions put forward in this debate are undoubtedly sometimes based on subjective childhood experiences, but we do not think their genesis or their validity can be reduced to these experiences.

Just like adults, children are a highly heterogeneous group with a wide variety of needs, interests, and life situations. There are very different ways of thinking about children and childhood, each shaped by normative expectations. This is particularly true of modern pluralistic societies, in which people with differing views of what is good and just live together, and in which social dissensus persists on many issues, including those concerning children. While some still believe in original sin, others aver that they no longer believe anything at all, and still others believe in science or whatever they may attribute to the scientific enterprise.

An ethics of childhood that claims to provide objective criteria for what can be defined as a sufficiently good childhood must also deal with this fact of pluralism (John Rawls). Since questions of a good childhood are the subject of constant political controversy and there is no lack of social groups and actors who act as defenders of children and their interests, this inevitably raises, first, the question of the compatibility of a concept of a good childhood with pluralism. Second, it poses the inseparable question of whether and to what extent a particular, milieu-dependent concept of a good childhood can be elevated to a universal standard and imposed on representatives of other concepts.

Concerning the *first* point, the diversity of ideas about what constitutes a good childhood must be taken seriously. It is not necessary to draw on relevant historical experience (e.g. in the two German dictatorships) to realize that coercive state support and enforcement of a particular concept of a good childhood can have devastating consequences. The conception we propose must therefore navigate between the Scylla of overly restricting a legitimate plurality of conceptions of childhood and the Charybdis of an arbitrary definition of what characterizes a good childhood. The latter cannot be plausible for the simple reason that the criteria named in this definition would themselves be arbitrary, leading to the absurd conclusion that all childhoods are equally good (because there are no nonarbitrary criteria of goodness). On the other hand, overly restricting possible points of view concerning childhood is not compatible with the legal leeway that parents can claim for themselves in dealing with their children. A good childhood must also be possible within the framework of a variety of different upbringings as well as diversity of family and living arrangements. In other words, there is—and here we can also take our cue from the relevant research—not just one correct form of childrearing (Berger & Fend, 2019). There are very different ways of organizing family life (Euteneuer & Uhlendorff, 2020) and correspondingly, of course, a plurality of ways of life into which children can be initiated.

Taking this plurality seriously does not mean advocating arbitrariness, nor does it absolve us from the task of critically examining this plurality. After all, defining criteria for a good childhood inevitably also means limiting plurality and determining when certain practices and arrangements should no longer be recognized as part of a legitimate spectrum of good childhoods. This also applies to the so-called liberal perfectionist conception presented below,[4] which is based on, among other things, the central and controversial value of personal autonomy. This conception excludes educational practices that indoctrinate children and considers such practices incompatible with a good childhood. Children who are not respected as people deserving of explanations and justifications for how they are treated, who are denied alternatives to their parents' way of life, and who are prevented from having the opportunity to ask questions of themselves and their parents, will not only have difficulties in dealing critically with their adopted way of life in later years. They will also be deprived of a central component of a good childhood. This does not mean that the parents' way of life has to be devalued entirely, of course. There is ample discussion to be had concerning the implications of autonomy as a central value for political policies that focus on the well-being of children. However, we are skeptical of justificatory approaches (such as certain variants of Rawlsian political liberalism) which, in the name of pluralism and state neutrality, leave too much leeway in the evaluation of children's lives, not least because these approaches do not always ground their claims in children's welfare, but in parents' interests or the binding customs of communities. While neutrality arguments can claim a certain plausibility with regard to adults, who are generally able to determine the shape and content of their own lives, this only applies to children to a very limited extent. They are not yet fully capable of this self-determination, as they first have to find out for themselves what a good life means to them in the long run (Fowler, 2020). We assume that an appropriate conception of a good childhood, which focuses primarily on the well-being of children, must take a stand on controversial political and ethical issues and draw on socially and politically controversial premises. Such an approach always faces the suspicion

[4] Liberal perfectionists advocate comprehensive liberalism, for example in the tradition of Kant and Mill: "(T)hey relate liberal commitments in political philosophy to some vision or conception of what matters in life and of the human person and its place in the world" (Waldron, 2004, p. 91). Representatives of politically liberal conceptions in the tradition of Rawls, on the other hand, claim to be able to justify their positions independently of such comprehensive doctrines: Nussbaum (2011).

that a culturally constituted conception of the good life of and for children is being generalized and imposed on other groups. There is no doubt that every conception of a good life for children is based on principles that are either supported or denied by other social groups. In fact, this is standardly the case, but it does not imply that such principles are impossible to justify. Rather, the idea is that all groups should ask themselves whether they acknowledge and incorporate the relevant core elements of a good childhood we outline below, particularly when they impose these conceptions of childhood on their children.

Before we present the core elements of a good childhood in detail, we will summarize the starting points and guiding principles on which our ethical case is based.

First, we start from the liberal perfectionist premise that personal autonomy is both intrinsically and instrumentally valuable for children and adults, since without the developed ability to critically reflect on the world, oneself and one's social relations in modern societies, individuals will hardly be able to lead a good life. In this way, we distinguish ourselves from political liberal approaches, which only provide for the obligatory implementation of the development of political autonomy for children, that is, autonomy with regard to political matters, in order to give parents and their conceptions of the good as much leeway as possible in education.

Second, since we do not assume that all childhood goods can be understood and justified solely in terms of their importance for the development of personal autonomy, we also proceed from substantive normative assumptions about a good childhood life and well-being, which we systematize in the form of objectively, intrinsically, and instrumentally valuable childhood goods (such as relational and educational goods). We thus distance ourselves from both subjectivist and other more objectivist conceptions, such as the capability approach, which in our view is too vague to provide sufficient orientation for the definition of a good childhood. Contrary to variants of ethical naturalism, as advocated above all in neo-Aristotelian conceptions, references to the nature of the child do not play a fundamental justificatory role in our conception of childhood for the reasons already mentioned. We are also skeptical of attempts to raise some notion of flourishing to the standard for optimal child development (Wolbert et al., 2021). While we believe that no conception of a good childhood can do without assumptions of appropriate development, and share several premises with such approaches (such as the role of intrinsic goods of childhood), we emphasize other points about child life.

The discovery and recognition of central goods of childhood are themselves the product of historical learning processes, which we interpret, *third*, as moral progress in dealing with children. This progress, in our view, should be defended, preserved, and enforced. The goods of childhood and the claims to validity associated with them open up possibilities for criticizing deficits affecting children and determining standards for determining progressive and regressive developments in the interpretation and shaping of childhood. This progress is of course not complete. Normative conceptions of childhood like the one we provide are also capable of 'learning' in the sense that they are a part of a collective learning process that can be traced back through the centuries to changes in social norms and empirical findings about children.

A characteristic difference between liberal perfectionist justifications and other justificatory approaches is therefore, *fourth*, their openness to empirical research. In other words, we consider our normative argument to be revisable based on empirical findings.

Fifth, we assume that central normative orientations, which flow into the formulation of the goods of childhood, violate standard liberal requirements of neutrality, but can nevertheless be based on a more or less broad consensus in liberal democratic societies, since these goods themselves are likely to be an expression of liberal democratic values. Of course, there are still parents and communities who believe that their children are their property and that beating children regularly is an effective educational tool. However, we hope that such views are becoming increasingly rare, not least because they are generally frowned upon and cannot be justified in the normative terms of the public conversation.

Sixth and finally, the conception of childhood presented here is offered as a contribution to democratic discourse. This means that any form of implementation or application of the conception remains dependent on political justification in democratic procedures.

References

Anderson, J., & Claassen, R. (2012). Sailing alone: Teenage autonomy and regimes of childhood. *Law and Philosophy, 31*(5), 495–522.

Andresen, S. (2005). *Einführung in die Jugendforschung*. Wissenschaftliche Buchgesellschaft.

Andresen, S., Neumann, S., & Public, K. (Eds.). (2018). *Kinder in Deutschland 2018: 4. World Vision Studie*. Beltz.

Archard, D. (2015). *Children. Rights and Childhood*. Routledge.
Baader, M. (2004). Der romantische Kindheitsmythos und seine Kontinuitäten in der Pädagogik und in der Kindheitsforschung. *Zeitschrift für Erziehungswissenschaft, 7*, 416–430.
Baader, M. (2015). Vulnerable Kinder in der Moderne in erziehungs- und emotionsgeschichtlicher Perspektive. In S. Andresen, C. Koch, & J. König (Eds.), *Vulnerable Kinder: Interdisziplinäre Annäherungen* (pp. 79–101). Springer.
Berger, F., & Fend, H. (2019). *Die Erfindung der Erziehung: Eine Einführung in die Erziehungswissenschaft*. Kohlhammer.
Betz, T., & Andresen, S. (Eds.). (2014). Child Well-Being: Potenzial und Grenzen eines Konzepts. Zeitschrift für Pädagogik, 60(4), 499–504.
Betz, T. (2022). Leitbilder "guter Kindheit". Retrieved May 23, 2023, from https://www.bpb.de/shop/zeitschriften/apuz/kinder-und-politik-2022/506635/leitbilder-guter-kindheit
Betz, T., & Andresen, S. (Eds.). (2014). Child Well-Being: Potenzial und Grenzen eines Konzepts. *Zeitschrift für Pädagogik, 60*(4), 499–504.
Betz, T., & Eßer, F. (2016). Kinder als Akteure—Forschungsbezogene Implikationen des erfolgreichen Agency-Konzepts. *Diskurs. Kindheits- und Jugendforschung*, (3), 301–314.
Betzler, M. (2021). The moral significance of adolescence. *Journal of Applied Philosophy*. https://doi.org/10.1111/japp.12556
Betzler, M. (2022). *The value of childhood* [Unpublished manuscript].
Brando, N. (2023). The moral relevance of social categories: Analysing the case of childhood. *European Journal of Philosophy, 31*, 195–208.
Bühler-Niederberger, D. (2020). *Lebensphase Kindheit* (2nd ed.). Beltz.
Dornes, M. (2012). *Die Modernisierung der Seele: Kind—Familie—Gesellschaft*. Fischer.
Dornes, M. (2014). *Die emotionale Welt des Kindes*. Fischer.
Euteneuer, M., & Uhlendorff, U. (2020). *Familie und Bildungsalltag als Bildungsherausforderung*. Beltz.
Felder, F. (2022). *The ethics of inclusive education*. Routledge.
Fowler, T. (2020). *Liberalism, Justice and Childhood*. Bristol University Press.
Giesinger, J. (2009). Neurodidaktik und die Normativität des Lernens. *Pädagogische Rundschau, 5*, 527–538.
Giesinger, J. (2019). Kinder und Erwachsene: Abgrenzungs- und Zuordnungsprobleme. In J. Drerup & G. Schweiger (Eds.), *Handbuch Philosophie der Kindheit* (pp. 43–49). Metzler.
Gopnik, A. (2009). *The Philosophical Baby*. Picador.
Gopnik, A. (2016). *The Gardener and the Carpenter*. Vintage.
Honneth, A., Maiwald, K.-O., Speck, S., & Trautmann, F. (Eds.). (2022). *Normative Paradoxien*. Campus.

Malone, K., Tesar, M., & Arndt, S. (2020). *Theorising Posthuman Childhood Studies*. Springer.

Matthews, G. (2009). Philosophy and developmental psychology: Outgrowing the deficit conception of childhood. In H. Siegel (Ed.), *The Oxford handbook of philosophy of education* (pp. 162–176). Oxford University Press.

Nussbaum, M. (2011). Perfectionist liberalism and political liberalism. *Philosophy and Public Affairs, 39*(1), 3–45.

Pinker, S. (2011). *The better angels of our nature: The decline of violence in history and its causes*. Allen Lane.

von Rosenberg, F. (2022). *Die beschädigte Kindheit: Das Krippensystem der DDR und seine Folgen*. C.H. Beck.

Rutschky, K. (Ed.). (1977). *Schwarze Pädagogik*. Ullstein.

Sidorenko, E. (2015). Book review of childism: Confronting prejudice against children. *Journal of Playwork Practice, 2*, 245–247.

Tenorth, H.-E. (2003). Pädagogik der Gewalt: Zur Logik der Erziehung im Nationalsozialismus. *Jahrbuch für historische Bildungsforschung, 9*, 7–31.

Tomasello, M. (2020). *Mensch werden: Eine Theorie der Ontogenese*. Suhrkamp.

Turmel, A. (2008). *A historical sociology of childhood*. Cambridge University Press.

Waldron, J. (2004). Liberalism, political and comprehensive. In G. Gaus & C. Kukathas (Eds.), *Handbook of political theory* (pp. 89–99). Sage.

Wall, J. (2022). From childhood studies to childism: Reconstructing the scholarly and social imaginations. *Children's Geographies, 20*, 257–270.

Winkler, M. (2017). *Kindheitsgeschichte*. Vandenhoeck & Ruprecht.

Wolbert, L., de Ruyter, D., & Schinkel, A. (2021). The flourishing child. *Journal of Philosophy of Education, 55*, 698–709.

Wulf, C. (2001). *Einführung in die Anthropologie der Erziehung*. Beltz.

Young-Bruehl, E. (2012). *Childism: Confronting prejudice against children*. Yale University Press.

Zinnecker, J. (2000). Kindheit und Jugend als pädagogisches Moratorium. In *Zeitschrift für Pädagogik. 42. Beiheft* (pp. 36–68). Beltz Verlag.

Zirfas, J. (2021). *Pädagogische Anthropologie*. Ferdinand Schöningh.

CHAPTER 3

Core Elements of a Good Childhood

The following reconstruction and definition of a good childhood is concerned with clarifying what constitutes a sufficiently good, not an ideal childhood. The core elements of a good childhood that we name below define minimum and necessary requirements for assessing a childhood as better or worse. We are not interested in constructing ideal worlds or utopian ideal states, but in identifying realistic possibilities for improvement, for understanding what belongs to a childhood that is *good enough*. The core elements of a good childhood can be pieced together in different ways and various priorities can be set. However, if not all requirements are met to a minimum extent, one cannot speak of a sufficiently good childhood. We thus take a sufficiency-oriented, threshold-based position, which assumes that a good childhood is characterized by the sufficient realization of objectively valuable childhood goods that are suitable for the absolute and comparative assessment of children's well-being. With the help of these goods, we show that children's rights, their claims to justice, and the associated duties of adults toward children can be established (such as a right to basic education). However, we should recognize that the childhood goods we name are not all distributed in the same way, nor can they all be easily codified in law (such as love, even if there have been attempts to establish a "right to be loved" (Liao, 2015); cf. Chaps. 4 and 5).

J. Drerup, G. Schweiger, *What is a Good Childhood?*,
https://doi.org/10.1007/978-3-031-74237-8_3

In the following, we present our approach to understanding childhood and provide a brief overview of the core elements of a good childhood. After doing so, we explain each of the individual goods in more concrete terms (Sects. 3.1–3.5). The core elements of a good childhood can be divided into four types of childhood goods: material goods (Sect. 3.1), relational goods (Sect. 3.2), educational goods (Sect. 3.3), and intrinsic goods of childhood (Sect. 3.4). In this account, the good of personal autonomy plays a special role as a meta-good of childhood, which to a certain extent supervenes on the different types of goods and their legitimate realization (Sect. 3.5). This catalogue of goods is to be understood as a proposal for analytical classification that is intended to enable a holistic assessment of what makes a childhood good. Empirical overlaps between forms of realization and the reciprocal facilitation of these goods are likely to be the rule, and concerning their precise normative allocation problems cannot always be avoided. This should not undermine the account proposed as long as one does not have exaggerated expectations of conceptual precision, expectations which are likely to be inappropriate to the complexity of the object of analysis. Here is the list of childhood goods on which our approach is based:

Material goods comprise the basic material requirements for a good childhood:

- These include provision of basic material goods that are necessary for the material security of children's basic needs, adequate nutrition, physical safety and integrity, health, play, learning opportunities, and a home.

Relational goods refer to the social relations and patterns of emotional relationship without which children cannot have a good childhood:

- These include love, care and attention; secure, trusting, and sufficiently reliable relationships, friendships, and forms of social participation.

Educational goods are those goods that are required to impart the knowledge and skills necessary for a good childhood in order to enable the appropriate cognitive, emotional, and social development of children:

- These include basic education, various opportunity structures for valuable learning and educational experiences, as well as physical, creative, and aesthetic experiences.

Intrinsic goods of childhood are those goods that are inherent in the specific abilities and characteristics of children's experiences and contribute to the realization of a good childhood:

- These include unplanned time, free and structured play; joyful, unregulated, and experimental forms of social interaction; a certain light-heartedness; and experiences with and in nature.

Personal autonomy as a meta-good of childhood not only is valuable in itself and necessary for a good childhood but also regulates and limits the legitimacy and appropriateness of how the other goods of childhood are enacted in social and pedagogical contexts. For our purposes, personal autonomy entails:

- Respect and esteem for the individuality and emerging autonomy of the child; autonomy-oriented forms of education and relationships that enable self-confidence, self-esteem, and self-respect.

Taken together, these are the goods that children need in order to lead a sufficiently good life. To reiterate, these goods must be guaranteed in order to ensure their well-being. In their capacity as threshold concepts, they are all *constitutive* goods of childhood, that is, they are equally important, and they are both necessary and sufficient for qualifying a childhood as good. Falling short of the minimum requirements with regard to one of the goods cannot be compensated for by exceeding these requirements for other goods. Such excesses can in some cases be seen as *contributing to* a good childhood. However, this does not necessarily have to be the case, especially if such excesses are accompanied by collateral damage to other goods (e.g. if children spend too much time playing freely and the realization of basic educational goods is neglected). Decisions about when exactly the relevant thresholds are reached are always based on value judgments. For example, one can argue about how exactly basic education should be defined and measured, what the necessary curricular constituents of basic education are, and what can perhaps be neglected. But while there are shades of gray and boundary cases, there are also black-and-white cases. Not every case is a boundary case. For example, it is incontrovertible that children who can neither read nor write at the age of 12 have fallen below a minimum threshold. That said, when resources are scarce for whatever reason, it may be necessary to weigh up the constitutive goods of childhood and set priorities. This also applies to the meta-good of personal autonomy, which should not be misunderstood as a *master value*. That is, its status as a meta-good does not mean it outweighs all other goods in terms of relevance and value (Sect. 3.5).

All childhood goods can be regarded as instrumental and intrinsically valuable. The instrumental value of these goods flows from the normative and empirical interdependencies between them. For example, those who cannot read (an educational good) will at some point no longer be able to participate in certain childhood games (an intrinsic good). Moreover, the instrumental value of childhood goods derives from their importance for children after childhood. Beyond this, childhood goods also have an intrinsic value, that is, they are valuable for the childhood phase of life itself, which is no less important than other phases of life. The intrinsic good of childhood play is, for example, not only valuable because it promotes the social skills necessary for success in the labor market. Likewise, autonomy is not only important because it allows one to critically self-reflect on one's choice of vocation. Despite the emphasis on children's present lives advocated, for instance, in different conceptions and doctrines of progressive education, we should not forget the future relevance of these goods—particularly, the individual and social costs that bad childhoods produce. We also believe that the potential conflicts between the present and the future should not be exaggerated. With regard to the basic goods we propose, such conflicts are only likely to be relevant to a very limited extent, since it is difficult to see why, for example, the provision of educational goods, intrinsic childhood goods, or personal autonomy in children's *present* lives should necessarily be in tension with an appropriate consideration of their *future* needs (and vice versa). At the same time, many aspects of a good childhood life are also good for adults, even if a good childhood does not guarantee a good adult life (but at least makes it more likely; see for empirical research on the probabilistic relationship between different forms of depravations during childhood and their negative long-term repercussions for the lives of adults; Dornes, 2014).

We also assume that the goods of childhood are *objectively* valuable for children. They are to be understood as goals that manifest themselves in concrete states and practices. 'Objective' here does not mean that they are somehow connected to 'eternal' truths. A theory of good childhood must also remain adaptable and revisable, that is, be able to react to changing social developments in childhood and to new results of empirical research on childhood. Objectivity for our purposes is to be understood in a weaker sense: Childhood goods are objectively valuable in the sense that, all else being equal and according to our present state of knowledge, they in fact improve the quality of life for *all* children (even if the focus here is on Western societies), because it is true for *all* children that they are deprived of central dimensions of a good childhood life if these goods are not realized. In other words, if one of the goods is completely or significantly lacking in a given childhood, it would not be a sufficiently good childhood, but a childhood deficient in this respect (e.g. a childhood without the intrinsic goods of childhood or without basic education). Deciding and justifying this statement is not a question of mere subjective taste (subjectivism) or arbitrary assumptions (relativism). Childhood goods are also not subjective in the sense that they only apply on the basis of children's views, for example because they correspond to their subjective well-being. Such views, which are reconstructed in empirical social research on children's well-being (see, for instance: Betz & Andresen, 2014; Andresen et al., 2018; Heite & Magyar-Haas, 2023, as well as the theoretical reflections of: Raghavan & Alexandrova, 2015) are largely in line with the list of goods we have provided and thus provide additional support and justification for our approach. However, a conception of a good childhood cannot be based solely on children's assessments, since children are generally not yet sufficiently informed about their interests. From this perspective, there would be little opportunity to criticize children's questionable adaptive preferences or assertions of consent (e.g. in the context of sexual abuse, where some of the perpetrators have made such assumptions). This requires objective standards that connect foundational values and norms to the relevant empirical research (e.g. on children's health). This in no way means that the subjective perspective and subjective happiness of children would not play a role in the justification of goods. Even if a good childhood cannot be reduced to a childhood that is subjectively perceived as happy, it can be assumed that the goods of childhood will in fact make the vast majority of children happy overall and are conducive to their subjective well-being. Even if a good childhood is not always a happy childhood and this cannot always be *guaranteed* by the goods of childhood, their realization can make happiness and, above all, the *preservation of children's ability to be happy* more likely. All this points to problems of implementation and realization, since the goods of childhood can be specified and interpreted in very different ways.

3.1 Material Goods

By material goods, we mean all those fundamental goods that are necessary for the material security of children's basic needs (adequate nutrition, physical safety and integrity, health, opportunities to play and learn, and a home of their own). We are aware of the many difficulties posed by the concept of basic needs, not least because they have always been culturally shaped and historically contingent and can serve as easy objects of criticism (e.g. for being colored by elitism or consumerism). We assume that children's basic needs are also anchored in anthropology—for example, in the physical nature and particular physical vulnerability of children. Material childhood goods are normatively relevant because they make a good childhood possible in modern societies. If a child comes to school hungry, its basic needs are not met. We should criticize this state of affairs because coming to school hungry is bad for the child's life. Despite all sociocultural variance and historical contingency, it is possible to distinguish between culturally specific preferences and tastes and what is fundamentally important for all children. For example, adequate nutrition, physical safety, integrity, and health, as well as a roof over one's head are important for all children, full stop. And despite all the difficulties that arise when categorizing true and false needs, there is also room for meaningful and legitimate discussion when it comes to the manipulation of children's needs, that is, the way these needs are created or the commercialization of educational spaces (such as advertising in schools). Thus, we should criticize when children's needs are preformed by interested actors in such a way that causes children to neglect their basic needs themselves or the realization of other childhood goods (be these intrinsic childhood goods or the meta-good of autonomy). At the same time, we must be wary of overly flippant and one-sided criticisms of consumerism that often portray children as merely passive victims of manipulation and do not take into account the special and often ambivalent characteristics of (digital) consumer cultures and commercialization, especially with respect to educational relationships and adult-child authority (e.g. the fewer opportunities for adults to control children's experiences).

In the end, such questions are of secondary importance when it comes to the question of the adequate provision of material childhood goods.

There is no doubt that, in affluent societies, the well-intentioned practice of showering children with toys can have other effects than the desired ones. However, it is also important to realize that having virtually no toys, opportunities to play or intellectual stimulation is deeply detrimental to children. Even if play and learning opportunities can be conducted very differently depending on cultural context, there are minimum requirements that must be met. After all, it makes a real difference whether you have a reasonably quiet place to do homework or not, whether you only have a single teddy bear or a wider range of toys. To put it succinctly: You can't buy a good childhood, but without the money needed to support a family, you can't have a good childhood either (Butterwegge & Butterwegge, 2021).

Material childhood goods cannot be externalized merely as *general prerequisites* or *enabling conditions* for a good childhood. They are *components* of a good childhood. Despite all the critical talk of excessive consumption, basic material childhood goods are not sufficiently available for many children, even in Western democracies. Children afflicted by these conditions not only have *less access* to material childhood goods than others, but *too few* of them.

For these reasons, child poverty remains a major sociopolitical problem with serious consequences. The COVID pandemic in particular revealed how important schools in the US are for providing for the nutrition of broad sections of the population (around half of American children are entitled to reduced-price or free school meals; Levinson, 2020). The loss of this crucial site of basic provision, in turn, highlighted the persistent socioeconomic inequalities in the US, inequalities that also exist—albeit in a less-severe form—in Germany. Beyond this, childhood poverty has consequences for social and cultural participation, educational opportunities, and the psychophysical health of children (Butterwegge, 2020; Schweiger, 2020). Poverty also negatively impacts children's developing self-understanding, particularly because they are confronted with various forms of social exclusion and face existential fears associated with a precarious form of life (Andresen et al., 2018). It is therefore hardly surprising that the subjective well-being of children often correlates with the socioeconomic status of their parents (Andresen, 2015), and that family instability and constant stress (with all its consequences for children) are more often a problem for socially disadvantaged families than for those for whom the provision of material childhood goods is a matter of course (Van der Kolk, 2014). Even if positive developments can be diagnosed in this area over the last few decades (Pinker, 2011), "it is still true," as Doris Bühler-Niederberger (2020, p. 25) puts it, that "as the victim statistics and corresponding studies show—(...) children (are) the most victimized population group. What is alarming is not only the high level of violence, but also the frequency with which it is not acknowledged." It should also be alarming to see how long the relevant circumstances (such as the sexual abuse of children) have been kept quiet, leaving children alone with the horror of an objectively bad childhood characterized by experiences of violence.

In short, the adequate provision of material childhood goods cannot be replaced or compensated for by other childhood goods, or only to a very limited extent. A lack of material goods also impairs access to other childhood goods.

3.2 Relational Goods

By relational goods, we mean all the emotionally anchored social relationships that ought to be realized in the lives of all children to a sufficient extent so that their lives can be called good (Gheaus, 2022). It is indisputable—and the relevant empirical research provides clear evidence of this (such as attachment research and developmental psychology in general; Ahnert, 2004; Dornes, 2014; see also the reflections of Hooks, 2001)—that children need love, care, and attention, as well as trusting, sufficiently secure, and reliable relationships from an early age. Without these relationships, they cannot develop appropriately. As genuinely dependent and vulnerable social beings who are at the mercy of their caregivers, children need affection and appreciation. It makes a radical difference to their lives whether they are treated with warmth and experience emotional support and care, or whether they are treated with indifference, aggression, and hostility. It is also relevant whether they are exploited by adults for their needs or whether an attempt is made to take seriously their authentic needs, their inner constitution, their worries and fears, and to help them to gradually understand and articulate these better. This is another reason to welcome the trend toward an increasing humanization of parent–child relationships and other pedagogical relationships, a process that becomes particularly apparent when viewed from a historical perspective (Berger & Fend, 2019, p. 102). We know today, or should know, that without the realization of these relational goods, children are not able to build a desirable healthy relationship to self, or can do so only with great difficulty.

This, too, impairs their current and future capacity for autonomy (Sect. 3.5).

At the same time, relational goods also have important consequences for children's own social relations and their understanding of how the social world works. Social relationship patterns always have an epistemic, that is, knowledge-related component. The way in which children are treated conveys an image of the social world and what can be expected of it. Children internalize such images of themselves and their social environment (Brumlik, 2019, p. 284, with reference to the results of attachment research) without usually having any means of reflectively correcting them. The relevance of such images for a good childhood is particularly evident when they become radically distorted. Children whose childhoods are characterized by dysfunctional relationships, pathological attachments, insecurity, anxiety, constant psychological stress, aggression, or violence are more prone to self-destructive behavior, a lack of self-esteem, and deficient self-regulation (Van der Kolk, 2014).

Cultivating relational goods does not mean that children should never be confronted with social conflicts or problems. However, it is important that this happens in an age-appropriate way and that children are offered approaches to dealing with conflicts in a civilized and constructive manner. A completely conflict- and friction-free childhood is not only an unrealistic idea, but also does not adequately prepare children for the conflicts and challenges that will inevitably arise later in life.

Equally important are the relational goods that manifest themselves in friendships and other forms of social participation. Children who are unable to experience friendships with their peers (or who primarily have negative and discouraging experiences) and are therefore unable to develop the ability to form friendships miss out on a central component of a good childhood (on this: Brumlik, 2019 as well as Berger & Fend, 2019). This finding should come as no surprise because empirical research on the good life of adults comes to very similar conclusions (Waldinger & Schulz, 2023). Even if childhood research shows how children create their own imaginary worlds, the ability to form friendships remains dependent on learning processes and opportunity structures that children cannot create all by themselves.

In this book, we do not want to make excessively controversial assumptions about the status and legitimacy of the family (Chap. 4). There is considerable diversity in how we can organize family and nonfamily ties to benefit children. In fact, the relational goods mentioned above have a greater chance of being realized when children regularly encounter a variety of caregivers and their associated relationship patterns. The assumption that parents and only parents are the ideal caregivers for their children is merely a traditional prejudice.

Historical childhood studies have shown that the growing attention paid to children as a specific social group was accompanied by their exclusion from many areas of public life. How one frames this diagnosis normatively is highly debatable, as is the question of what conclusions one draws from such a diagnosis for the legitimate shaping of the relationship between children and adults. Here, too, one should be wary of making exaggerated, normatively absolute judgments. The exclusion of children through the creation of specialized institutions (like schools) is not just disadvantageous; they also offer new forms of social participation. These opportunities for participation—from museums, workshops, and leisure parks, to opportunities for political engagement—certainly have their place, just as some of the more awkward attempts to fuse the child and adult worlds are better abandoned. Well-organized, child-specific institutions can be seen as valuable precisely because they remove children from the hardships, disappointments, and risks of participation in adult life. This does not rule out that children can be allowed to participate in public life in their own unique ways. In any case, what is probably uncontroversial in this controversy is that a totally privatized, isolated, and world-free childhood, so to speak—that is, a childhood completely separate from public-related activities—lacks significant opportunities for rich social experience. What seems most important to us is that there must be an appropriate range of desirable options for meaningful and significant social participation for children.

As goods of childhood, relational goods can be realized in many different ways, just as they manifest themselves in many different role constellations and carry with them varying requirements (e.g. one can expect love from parents, but one should not expect this from teachers). However, relational goods cannot be substituted by other goods of childhood (such as material goods or educational goods). As with material goods, their absence cannot be compensated for, since their lack of realization inevitably results in a deficient childhood in this respect.

3.3 Educational Goods

Educational goods are those goods that are necessary for imparting the knowledge and skills required for a good childhood. These goods support the appropriate cognitive, emotional, and social development of children. Educational goods include, above all, basic education, that is, the process by which children acquire a set of basic cultural competencies (such as basic reading-, writing-, mathematical competencies). According to Tenorth (2020), basic education provides the basic prerequisites for social participation in modern societies and offer a sufficiency-oriented standard of educational justice. Without these basic cultural skills, higher forms of education or *Bildung* (whatever one may associate with these terms) are hardly conceivable. Moreover, their absence makes it much more difficult to lead a good life in modern societies. Basic cultural competencies open up opportunities for independent interaction with oneself and the world. Children learn to read and sculpt their own aesthetic experiences; they learn to solve problems in the real world, and to do so independently of adults and their pedagogical ambitions. Such experiences are important for the development of independence and personal autonomy and for the realization of other goods of childhood, not least because lacking basic education can also lead to social exclusion. Despite all the legitimate disputes about the definition and canonization of educational standards and curricula, it is nothing less than scandalous that a large number of children leave elementary school without receiving a basic education in many societies across the globe.

However, the educational goods that are fundamental to a good childhood do not only include basic cultural competencies. Educational goods also include basic historical, political, religious, and scientific knowledge; valuable educational experiences (such as sports, creative activities, and aesthetic pursuits); and participation in meaningful extracurricular activities. It seems to us to be a rather 'uneducational' assumption to assume that education only takes place in designated institutions of education. A childhood in which educational experiences are limited solely to the school environment would be just as 'world-free' as a childhood in which basic education is absent.

At the same time, educational goods understood in this way can only fulfill their function as core elements of a sufficiently good childhood if (1) the requirements of an autonomy-oriented education are respected (see Sect. 3.5) and (2) certain epistemic, scientific, and political standards are observed when they are conveyed (Chap. 5). This means that the selection of educational content must be tied back to the centrality of systematic, academic knowledge and to the fundamental political values of democratic societies (Drerup, 2021). Children who are told from an early age that homosexuality is unnatural and that racism is a legitimate political view, who are told that they will suffer agony if they do not adhere to the authority of the holy scriptures, or who are punished if they do not blindly follow the political doctrines of their parents—are given an epistemically and politically distorted picture of the social world. Such worldviews are often, although not always, likely to have a negative impact on the life of the child (not to mention the lives of other children) and stands to undermine their self-understanding as self-determining and autonomous individuals.[1] We do not want to deny that children of religious fundamentalists and right-wing radicals can also have a good childhood in certain respects. However, we are committed to the plausible premise that such ideological exploitations of children and childhood are in many cases accompanied by pedagogical practices and arrangements that cannot be reconciled with the pedagogically legitimate realization of educational and other goods of childhood (see: Tenorth, 2003; Simon & Thole, 2021).

3.4 Intrinsic Goods of Childhood

The intrinsic goods of childhood are those goods that are inherent in the specific qualities and characteristics of children's experiences, and whose realization is therefore necessary for a good childhood. These include free and structured play; joyful, unregulated, and experimental forms of social interaction; a certain light-heartedness; and experiences with and in nature. Following neo-Romantic conceptions of childhood, one can argue that children have special access to these goods on account of their specific developmental abilities and characteristics, such as openness, curiosity, and the ability to wonder about the world and imagine alternative worlds. We consider this claim to be plausible because children are *indeed* particularly good at playing, creating their own worlds, and experiencing joy in a carefree way, at least if they are given sufficient opportunities to do so. Affirming this claim about children does not represent a romantic

[1] Even if moral and democratic education are not our topic here, it should be pointed out that depravations related to the good life and moral and political depravations often, if not always, go hand in hand.

projection that can be chalked up merely to unjust generational orders and power relations. The normative assumption that the intrinsic goods of childhood are valuable for children as children can also be justified independently of controversial anthropological assumptions specifically related to children. For example, there are good reasons to assume that many of the intrinsic goods of childhood are not only good for children, but are generally also good for adults. Even adult life is likely to be an impoverished one if such goods are absent (Gheaus, 2015). However, the value and normative status of intrinsic childhood goods is not identical for children and adults. Adults generally have greater scope to lead a life of their own choosing within a framework of social guidelines and restrictions. Children have this opportunity to a lesser extent.

The often-repeated critique that modern childhood is overly managed, controlled, and structured is also based on the assumption that a childhood without intrinsic goods is not a good childhood. It is therefore worth considering how we might evaluate a childhood *without* intrinsic goods: A childhood that offers no or hardly any opportunities for free play, for unregulated interaction with other children and adults, or that provides virtually no experiences of nature will not be sufficiently good to be called good. Children who are robbed of their light-heartedness at an early age because they are manipulated or oppressed by adults, who live in constant fear, or who are expelled from childhood at a very early age simply do not have a sufficiently good childhood.

Most children are likely to see it this way themselves. Whether our normative claims about the intrinsic goods of childhood amount to a 'social construction' or not is of secondary importance. Of course, it is also possible to argue for an alternative construction of childhood for which none of these goods would apply, but then the question becomes whether this construction is also ethically justified. Since every practical construction of childhood is accompanied by moral costs, we only advocate the sufficient realization of the intrinsic goods of childhood in the social domains relevant to children's lives (above all family, daycare, school, but also noninstitutional public domains). We do not argue for a radical expansion of the demands on caretakers to provide for a good childhood. For example, in the name of the intrinsic goods of childhood, one might wish for a return to a classic childhood 'on the streets' in order to ensure that children can once again move around freely and without supervision in cities. And one might also argue for the abolition of schools, assuming that children would then be able to enact the intrinsic goods of childhood in an unregulated and nonadministered way. However, this would also inevitably entail costs (such as traffic fatalities or functional illiteracy) that would ultimately have to be borne by children themselves. From a sufficiency-oriented view of a good childhood, intrinsic childhood goods describe a central value that is necessary for a good childhood and must therefore be realized to a sufficient extent, bearing in mind that children's opportunities to acquire these goods in their childhood are unevenly distributed. It is still the case that not all families are able to create appropriate opportunity structures for providing the intrinsic goods of childhood, often for socioeconomic reasons.

3.5 Autonomy as a Meta-Good of a Good Childhood

Describing personal autonomy as a meta-good of a good childhood means first and foremost that the realization of *all* childhood goods must also be guided by the requirements of an autonomy-oriented upbringing. Before the constitutive and corrective functions of this good are explained, the concept of autonomy itself must first be clarified.

Following the results of recent developmental psychological research, several philosophers have argued that young children have basic forms of autonomy that need to be taken seriously. This camp generally also rejects 'deficit conceptions' of childhood, such as those expressed in neo-Kantian conceptions of autonomy, whereby children are primarily considered not yet sufficiently capable of reasonable self-determination. In contrast to this view, researchers have shown that younger children cannot be considered irrational, self-centered, and amoral, but in certain respects are even more capable thinkers and actors than adults (e.g. their ability to imagine and learn; Gopnik, 2009). This empirical insight, which has also become increasingly accepted in various areas of life in recent decades (e.g. by involving children more in decisions and discussions and respecting them as individuals and persons; Dornes, 2012), has also found its way into philosophical theories of autonomy.

Amy Mullin (2007), for example, starts from the plausible assumption that autonomy can already be attributed to young children between the ages of three and eight. This is the *first* point of departure for the relational theory of autonomy our approach is based on. In her argument, she uses the distinction between global autonomy, which refers to one's entire way of life, and local autonomy, which only refers to certain areas of life. With this distinction, she shows that traditional views of autonomy should be revised, particularly when they assume that children are per se incapable of autonomous thought and action. Children do not, in fact, exhibit limited self-reflection skills, vulnerability, and social dependence in every domain of life. Even young children can cultivate volitional commitments, uphold intersubjective obligations, and demonstrate forms of care in their world, through which they assert—in their own way—what is important and valuable to them. These practices ought to be understood as an expression of their local autonomy, to be taken seriously and respected, which does not mean that they all have to be considered authoritative, nor that pedagogical revision is never justified. Given that some of the most popular theories of autonomy are based on questionable threshold conditions that even most adults are unlikely to meet, we can and should question the classical view that only certain forms of rationality and self-reflection can be regarded as a source of personhood and moral status (without disavowing them as *educational* aims). A distinction must be made here between developing child autonomy through educational practices and autonomy as an educational aim—one that prepares children for the challenges and responsibilities of adult status.

Following theories of relational autonomy, the development and realization of childhood autonomy is to be understood as a genuinely social phenomenon. This is our *second* point of departure. Children cannot develop the constitutive prerequisites of autonomy (self-confidence, self-respect and self-esteem) without certain forms of recognition (such as appreciation and love; see, for example: Honneth, 1994; Dornes, 2014). The fact that children's autonomy is enacted in social relationships and is inconceivable without them does not mean that children—despite their social vulnerability, dependence, and lack of independence—are not also to be understood as agents who are capable of individual autonomy to a limited extent.

Our *third* point of departure involves taking the self- and co-determination skills of even younger children seriously. In our view, doing so lays the foundations for the later development of autonomy in political matters. For this reason, it is hardly plausible to assume that the prerequisites for personal and political autonomy can be schematically separated from one another in the educational and socialization process. This is because the experience of co-determination and self-determination are always likely to have an impact on both public and political areas of life.

What is the relationship between local child autonomy and the other goods of childhood? What does this relationship mean for the *pedagogical realization* of a good childhood? It should be obvious that an education for autonomy without a sufficient guarantee of material childhood goods encounters enormous obstacles. The same also applies in cases when caretakers fail to provide central relational goods (such as love and respect) such that the development of the child's personal autonomy will be impaired; or when they withhold the provision of educational goods. Intrinsic childhood goods also open up important opportunities for children to develop autonomy (such as free and unregulated play). The other childhood goods thus not only provide important prerequisites for the development of autonomy. They can only be appropriately realized in educational terms if children's emerging autonomy is respected and they are granted sufficient scope for autonomous thought and action.

Education for autonomy is compatible with a plurality of different forms and cultures of education so long as these do not fall short of providing the core goods of childhood. Understanding autonomy as a meta-good of a good childhood therefore boils down to the following point: It makes a central difference *how* the goods of childhood are conveyed and enacted in each case. That is, it makes a difference whether children see that their interests and points of view are taken into account, whether one discusses courses of action *with* them and explains relevant contexts to them, whether they are involved in decisions about their lives, and, generally, whether they are taken seriously and respected as persons or not. Personal autonomy is therefore incompatible with radically control-oriented pedagogies, indoctrination, and the associated disregard for the nascent autonomy and individuality of children as persons. This means that autonomy-promoting education, in contrast to forms of education based solely on behavioral control and conditioning, must always be oriented toward acquiring reasoned insight and consent (Hügli, 1999). Despite all the difficulties associated with models of future and hypothetical consent (such as problems of the *self-fulfilling prophecy*), there are practices of upbringing and socialization (such as violent indoctrination and manipulation) that—if the children involved one day enlighten themselves about the way in which their internalized views have come about (see, the conception of autonomy developed by Christman, 2009)—can cause them to feel deeply alienated from their own selves. Forms of education that do not do justice to this biographical and diachronic dimension of autonomy are therefore just as illegitimate as those that seek to limit children's horizons to a single way of life and conception of the good. This is not to advocate a liberal supermarket model of autonomous self-selection, but to argue that even young children should be confronted with a plurality of perspectives and life possibilities, without which they cannot learn what it means to develop a conception of the good life that suits them.

Children's development of autonomy and its enactment are primarily mediated by more or less intelligent and flexible habits and social patterns. The way in which children begin to think about their lives is also strongly influenced by the opportunities and relations of dependency in which they live. They therefore need good role models to guide them, even if their parents do not take on this task themselves, and regardless of the doctrines that guide their parents in their lives. It is not per se illegitimate for parents to want to pass on their concept of a good life to their children, at least as long as they do not close off the possibility of an open future for their children in which they could also develop other views of a good life (Feinberg, 1980).

Despite the importance of autonomy in childhood, one must remain realistic with regard to what this can and cannot mean from a pedagogical perspective. After all, since autonomy does not represent the only core element of a good childhood and is closely interwoven with the other core elements, the establishment of paternalistic arrangements and practices aimed at realizing the other goods of childhood would not be illegitimate in itself. This is the case not least because it is relevant here *which* decisions are made by children, on what *basis* (e.g. knowledge, experience) they are made, with regard to *what conditions or goals* they are formulated, with what *consequences* they are connected in the decision context, and thus of what *quality* they happen to be. These aspects help adults determine whether children's judgments are, in the context in question, to be respected or not respected. Understanding personal autonomy as a constitutive meta-good thus has far-reaching consequences for the evaluation of a good childhood, but this does not mean that we should ignore the tensions associated with the pedagogical paradox expressed in Immanuel Kant's classic question, 'How do I cultivate freedom in the face of coercion?' Rather, personal autonomy as a meta-good has a constitutive and corrective function, with which different ways of enacting the goods of childhood can be put to the test. This allows us to assess whether the power asymmetries unavoidable in pedagogical contexts have been managed in a reasonable way. From this perspective, it is one-sided attempts to resolve the pedagogical paradox with overly coercive pedagogies on the one hand and laissez-faire pedagogies on the other that make autonomy the only standard of a good childhood. In our view, these approaches amount to a neglect and misrecognition of children's needs that should be criticized. Taking appropriate pedagogical account of children's autonomy therefore offers no reason to declare the difference in status between children and adults obsolete or normatively irrelevant, nor to impose the same responsibilities and tasks on children as on adults.

The shaping of a good childhood also remains a task for society as a whole. Accordingly, a good childhood cannot be adequately understood and guaranteed if the social conditions in which it is to be realized are not addressed. This primarily concerns the institutions—family and state—which often exist in a tense relationship with each other when defining, justifying, and enforcing the responsibilities, rights, and duties toward children. The five goods of childhood formulate minimum requirements for a good childhood to which all children have a moral and, in some cases, legal claim. They thus serve as a normative framework from which social developments incompatible with their enactment can be criticized. Based on the sufficiency-oriented approach advocated here, the focus is primarily placed on childhoods that are not good enough, with particular priority given to the most disadvantaged. Inequalities above the minimum conditions defined by the essential childhood goods are not completely irrelevant, but they do not represent the central problem of justice that we are highlighting in this book.

References

Ahnert, L. (Ed.). (2004). *Frühe Bindung*. Reinhardt.

Andresen, S. (2015). Das vulnerable Kind in Armut. In S. Andresen, J. König, & C. Koch (Eds.), *Vulnerable Kinder* (pp. 137–152). Springer VS.

Andresen, S., Neumann, S., & Public, K. (Eds.). (2018). *Kinder in Deutschland 2018: 4. World Vision Studie*. Beltz.

Berger, F., & Fend, H. (2019). *Die Erfindung der Erziehung: Eine Einführung in die Erziehungswissenschaft*. Kohlhammer.

Betz, T., & Andresen, S. (2014). Child Well-Being: Potenzial und Grenzen eines Konzepts. *Zeitschrift für Pädagogik, 60*(4), 499–504.

Brumlik, M. (2019). *Bildung und Glück* (2nd ed.). Europäische Verlagsanstalt.

Bühler-Niederberger, D. (2020). Warum es Kindheit nicht gibt. *Kursbuch, 201*, 24–40.

Butterwegge, C. (2020). *Die zerrissene Republik*. Bpb.

Butterwegge, C., & Butterwegge, C. (2021). *Kinder der Ungleichheit: Wie sich die Gesellschaft ihrer Zukunft beraubt.* Campus.

Christman, J. (2009). *The Politics of Persons.* Cambridge University Press.

Dornes, M. (2012). *Die Modernisierung der Seele: Kind–Familie—Gesellschaft.* Fischer.

Dornes, M. (2014). *Die emotionale Welt des Kindes.* Fischer.

Drerup, J. (2021). *Kontroverse Themen im Unterricht: Konstruktiv streiten lernen.* Reclam.

Feinberg, J. (1980). A child's right to an open future. In H. LaFolette & W. Aitken (Eds.), *Whose child? Parental rights, parental authority and state power* (pp. 124–153). Littlefield, Adams, and Co.

Gheaus, A. (2015). The intrinsic goods of childhood and the just society. In A. Bagattini & C. Macleod (Eds.), *The nature of children's well-being* (pp. 35–52). Springer.

Gheaus, A. (2022). *Personal relationship goods.* Retrieved May 23, 2023, from https://plato.stanford.edu/entries/personal-relationship-goods/.

Gopnik, A. (2009). *The philosophical baby.* Picador.

Heite, C., & Magyar-Haas, V. (Eds.). (2023). *Kindheit(en) im Blick zeitgenössischer Forschungen.* Springer VS.

Honneth, A. (1994). *Kampf um Anerkennung.* Suhrkamp.

Hooks, B. (2001). *All about love: New visions.* William Morrow.

Hügli, A. (1999). *Philosophie und Pädagogik.* WBG.

Levinson, M. (2020). Educational ethics during a pandemic. Retrieved June 1, 2020, from https://ethics.harvard.edu/files/center-for-ethics/files/17educationalethics.pdf

Liao, M. (2015). *The right to be loved.* Oxford University Press.

Mullin, A. (2007). Children, autonomy, and care. *Journal of Social Philosophy, 38*, 536–553.

Pinker, S. (2011). *The better angels of our nature: The decline of violence in history and its causes.* Allen Lane.

Raghavan, R., & Alexandrova, A. (2015). Toward a theory of child well-being. *Social Indicators Research, 121*, 887–902.

Schweiger, G. (2020). Warum Kinder arm sind. *Kursbuch, 201*, 61–76.

Simon, S., & Thole, W. (2021). Die braune Melange "konservativ-revolutionärer" Erziehung. In J. Sehmer, S. Simon, & J. Ten Jelsen (Eds.), *recht extrem? Dynamiken in zivilgesellschaftlichen Räumen* (pp. 227–240). Springer VS.

Tenorth, H.-E. (2003). Pädagogik der Gewalt: Zur Logik der Erziehung im Nationalsozialismus. *Jahrbuch für historische Bildungsforschung, 9*, 7–31.

Tenorth, H.-E. (2020). *Die Rede von Bildung: Tradition, Praxis, Geltung—Beobachtungen aus der Distanz.* J.B. Metzler.

Van der Kolk, B. (2014). *The body keeps the score.* Penguin Books.

Waldinger, R., & Schulz, M. (2023). *The good life and how to live it.* Penguin.

CHAPTER 4

Children, Parents, and Families

Now that we have outlined what goods make up a good childhood, let us turn to the question of who is responsible for ensuring that children have a good childhood. We will begin by clarifying what responsibilities *parents* have in providing a good childhood and bracket for now how the state enters in to these responsibilities. The family is a social institution that is embedded in state institutions and regulations (such as legal requirements). The ability of (many) parents to contribute to the realization of a good childhood is therefore limited by external sociopolitical and socioeconomic factors, in particular by material hardship and the precarious conditions in which they live. However, it does not follow from this interweaving of state, society, and family that the corresponding domains of responsibility cannot be separated from each other analytically or that parents could or should be relieved of responsibilities for a good childhood. Parental support is, in fact, necessary for the enactment of the goods of childhood.

But first a few explanations of the use of the terms 'family' and 'parents.' There is continuing debate on the definition and justification of parental rights and duties. Historical family research not only sheds light on the diversity of forms of human coexistence and family constellations beyond the bourgeois nuclear family (Mitterauer & Sieder, 1991). It also disproves various myths about the history of the family that have proven to be surprisingly resistant. These myths are often used to criticize

J. Drerup, G. Schweiger, *What is a Good Childhood?*,
https://doi.org/10.1007/978-3-031-74237-8_4

contemporary family relationships, which in many cases express a longing for premodern ways of life—for example, cohesive extended families, which as a rule hardly ever corresponded to the harmonious ideal image projected onto them (Mitterauer, 1991). Social scientific family research has also demonstrated the diversity of contemporary family models, their consequences for family relationships, and changing social conditions for shaping the family. These conditions include shifting role attributions and legal relationships in families, increasing public responsibility for children and their upbringing, as well as different ways of dealing with educational challenges in families (Euteneuer & Uhlendorff, 2020). The normative and empirical diversity of families found in pluralistic societies is also reflected in various conceptions of parenthood (Vaskovics, 2020). For example, a distinction can be made between legal parenthood, that is, those persons who are legally responsible for the child, and genetic parenthood, that is, those persons who are the child's genetic parents. A special case is gestational motherhood, where a woman who was pregnant with the child and gave birth to it is not the genetic mother because of an egg donation. Finally, there is social parenthood, that is, those people who actually look after and care for the child. These forms of parenthood often coincide, but this is by no means always the case. The classical nuclear family, consisting of parents who are a married couple and their genetic children for whom they also assume legal and social parenthood, has long since ceased to exist as the only viable option for children and their caretakers.

In the following, we assume that a good childhood can be enacted within the framework of a wide range of family forms and conceptions of parenthood. Despite all justified criticism, the institution of the family is the place where this should be possible. The idea of abolishing the family can be entertained, of course (Lewis, 2023), but our considerations must take into account the often-negative historical experiences associated with such agendas. Radical changes to the social organization of intergenerational relationships would hardly be always better for children and their normative rights and interests (Gheaus, 2018). From a liberal perspective, it is legitimate and sensible to discuss different experiments in living (John Stuart Mill) and to think about alternatives to the status quo. However, the relevant rights and interests of all parties must be taken into account.

Parents are primarily, if not solely, responsible for a good childhood for their children. The rights of parents to raise their children, and the power and control they are allowed to exercise over their children's lives, derive primarily from this responsibility. If parents are unable to do this or willfully do not want to give their children a good life, then they lose their parental rights (at least partially, but in severe cases also completely). This *child-centered*—as opposed to *parent-centered*—view is compatible with various ethical justifications of parental rights. It does justice to the primacy of the best interests of the child, even in the relationship between children's rights and the educational rights of parents. According to Giesinger (2015), a distinction can be made here between the right to assume the social parental role in the first place and the specific rights and duties that arise in the context of exercising the parental role. The former right can be regarded as a *fundamental* right, the latter as *derived* from the corresponding duties toward children. This distinction is important, as without fundamental parental rights one could argue that even sufficiently good parents who fulfill their duties could lose their rights, since there may be other parents who would be better suited for the task (which is generally not in the interests of the children). This would not take into account the fact that parents also have legitimate interests in dealing with their children, which expresses a significant life project for them. Even if we reject a purely parent-centered view and the associated strong legal and moral weighting of parents' interests toward their children, as is sometimes prevalent in the public and political debate, this does not mean that an appropriate balance cannot be struck between the interests and rights of parents and children. Children's interest and rights must, in our view, be given equal moral weight. However, this may not be possible if the legal and moral focus is placed only on parents or only on children. According to Giesinger, such a balance can be achieved by specifying more precisely what the duties of parents toward children are and which can be regarded as a condition for the legitimate *exercise* of parental rights. This means that the justification and specification of parental rights is based on the assumption that the duties to children's welfare *take precedence* over their own liberty rights qua parents (but not necessarily qua adult individuals). That is, parents have precisely the rights they need in relation to their children in order to enable the latter to lead a sufficiently good life.

In light of this conclusion, a second distinction is also relevant. The linking of parental rights to parental duties in the context of a child-centered perspective can be understood in a narrower legal sense and a broader moral sense. It would be implausible to argue that every failure to enact the goods of childhood due to parental misconduct should automatically have legal consequences. This is due to the fact that not all the goods of childhood can be easily translated into legally enforceable claims and that parent–child relationships cannot and should not be legalized in all their normative dimensions. This itself is likely to be associated with collateral damage for these relationships. Nor are children's rights alone sufficient to take into account the normatively relevant core elements of a good childhood in their entirety. Although they provide important opportunities for the political enforcement of children's interests, they are themselves in need of interpretation and application and can only provide limited normative guidance for the appropriate regulation and pedagogical shaping of parent–child relationships. It would therefore go too far and lead to a practically unhelpful inflation of rights if one were to attempt to tie *all* parental duties back to children's rights and justify them *only* by reference to them. Just as fundamental parental rights are, for good reasons, generally up for discussion, especially in cases of gross violations of children's welfare, parents also have a certain legal and moral leeway in the way in which they fulfill their duties toward their children as parents. Therefore, when we argue below that parental rights are linked to the sufficient enactment of the goods of childhood, the talk of rights here is to be understood in the broader sense of moral rights and duties. In other words, parents are bound to *more far-reaching* moral obligations toward their children than can be legally codified and enforced.

These moral obligations correspond to a conception of parenthood that is good enough for children and their lives. So here, too, we are not concerned with ideal images of good parenting or a good family, but with responsibilities and moral duties that can realistically be expected of all people who take on the role of parents. These can be spelled out along the lines of the five categories of childhood goods. It is in the nature of these goods that they are subject to varying degrees of parental control, and some of them cannot be guaranteed by parents alone. Rather, these goods are often dependent on the support of other actors, in particular the state and its institutions.

This is likely to be the case in particular with the *material goods of childhood*, since child poverty in the vast majority of cases follows family poverty. It is of course much more difficult for poor parents to secure basic childhood material goods for their children. Poorer families can also offer their children a good childhood, even if this presents an enormous challenge for parents in precarious life situations and support is required. However, if we do not want to disempower parents in their role as parents, we must accept that, despite such difficulties, it is the parents who bear the primary responsibility for ensuring that their children have sufficient material goods (adequate nutrition, health, etc.). We attribute this task to the responsibility of parents because it is an expression of a liberal society when parents take responsibility for themselves and their children. To be able to take care of oneself and one's children, also in material terms, is a source of respect and recognition in modern liberal societies.

Of course, the family offers a framework in which neglect, abuse, and violence are possible due to the privacy that the state grants and secures, and due to the physical and emotional closeness that family life and relationships entail. Unfortunately, the family is the most likely place for children to be victimized. Good parenting is incompatible with violent parenting and also incompatible with the visibility of violence between parents. Other forms of violation through insults, belittling, or even disrespect are often more subtle and less easily recognized, but they too are inconsistent with parental responsibility. Adults who claim parental status can and should be aware of this. Here, as with other childhood goods, the contexts and hardships that affect parents in different social situations in different ways must always be considered and critically examined.

Ensuring the adequate provision of *relational goods* that are enacted directly and exclusively in the parent–child relationship, such as love, care, trust, affection, and encouragement, are the sole responsibility of the parents. These goods are also likely to be central to a good life for most parents and are therefore also used to justify parental rights (Brighouse & Swift, 2014). Parents are capable of giving their children love, care, and affection in various ways, often due to their own attachment experiences as children. Here, too, it depends on social conditions as to how easy it is for parents to enact these relational goods. However, neither restrictive social conditions nor the fact that these goods cannot all be easily formalized in, for example, the form of a right to love, release parents from the obligation to take responsibility for these relational goods in their dealings with their children. Precisely because children are particularly vulnerable to and largely at the mercy of their parents in the family relationship, the latter are obliged to regulate their own emotional reactions toward their children.

With this position, we are not committing ourselves to more or less historically contingent ideological principles (e.g. maternal love; see on this: Badinter, 1991), but are merely stating that children cannot have a good childhood in families if they are not loved and given attention and care. Of course, parenthood can be exhausting, unfulfilling, tiring, and overwhelming. There can be phases in which parental freedom and self-realization are severely restricted. Even if a child-friendly society will try to reduce such tensions, it remains the responsibility of parents not to neglect their children and, when necessary, to curtail their own personal needs, interests, and freedoms for the good of their children. General references to unjust 'structures' are not enough to absolve parents of their individual responsibility toward their children. Even if one concedes that parents are not *just* parents and that their obligations toward their children are therefore limited, the sufficient enactment of relational goods in continuous and reliable relationships is a minimum requirement for good parenting. In other words, parental responsibilities cannot be (permanently) delegated, especially not to younger children, who would be wronged if they were prematurely committed to the role of providing emotional and practical care. The social fact that parents are capable of fulfilling this requirement in various ways, in conjunction with the fact that the bourgeois nuclear family can reproduce social pathologies, speaks in favor of trying to reduce the risks associated with the parental monopoly on childrearing. It encourages us as a society to provide the relevant relational goods at least partially outside of close family relationships. However, this in turn does not change the fact that it is ultimately the parents who are responsible for making use of external services.

Families can be regarded as educational environments of their own kind (see Winkler, 2012) in which *educational goods* are also imparted. Families offer young people formal skills and knowledge, which are particularly helpful for their route through the educational system, but they are also sites of informal education. While one of the main tasks of schools is to impart basic education, one of the central educational duties of parents is to grant children access to extracurricular educational experiences beyond their duty to provide suitable conditions for participating in formal education. Parents who are interested in neither one nor the other—where the reason for this lack of interest is ultimately of secondary importance—and who withhold a variety of educational experiences from their children are failing in their duty as parents to ensure a good childhood for their children. If parents do not (or cannot) adequately meet the requirements of the educational system, this provides legitimate grounds for criticism of structurally anchored social injustices, but this does not release parents from their education-related duties. Of course, we should not expect too much from parents in this respect, and expectations should be made as transparent and understandable as possible (El Mafaalani, 2021). But expecting nothing from them in relation to their children's education would be too little.

Ensuring the ***intrinsic goods of childhood*** in the context of the family means, above all, opening up opportunities for children to shape significant parts of their lives together with other children or adults, and to do so in relative independence from external societal expectations. Opening up an appropriate domain of independent action for children does not necessarily mean that one does not act pedagogically. Deliberately holding back one's pedagogical interventions as a parent can also be pedagogically motivated. In principle, the intrinsic goods of childhood are necessary for a good childhood, and parents are responsible for providing their children with the appropriate degree of freedom necessary to achieve them. The view propagated in modern conceptions of childhood that children are entitled to spaces and times in which they are relieved of obligations and responsibilities points to the need for a certain restraint when it comes to parental ambitions for their children. After all, good parents are also parents who know that they cannot and must not do everything with and for their child; nor can they guarantee that all the characteristics of a good childhood are fulfilled. This is why good (enough) parents also rely on external support, social infrastructure, and relevant expertise outside of the family.

If autonomy is to be enacted *as a meta-good of a good childhood* in the context of family education, children must be respected as individuals and persons with independent moral status. Educational arrangements, routines, and practices must be designed in a way that is compatible with children's current and future development of autonomy. Committing parents to such ethical standards of autonomy is a demanding requirement that corresponds to social developments in recent decades—from the paradigm of the controlling family to that of the family, where practices of negotiation and participation in decision-making form a central part of family life (Dornes, 2012). However, it also leads to subsequent conflicts with more traditionally oriented communities and parents, conflicts that are unavoidable in pluralistic societies.

Some clarification is needed with regard to these conflicts. On the one hand, children, especially younger children, are not yet finished personalities, and their development is always simultaneously the product of their own activity—of their own ideas and of the diverse influences upon them from their social environment. From an ethical point of view, it is therefore unreasonable to demand absolute neutrality from parents in moral or ideological questions. Parents cannot and should not discard their personality or their conception of the good when raising their children, not least because this would hardly be compatible with the enactment of the relevant relational goods (Brighouse & Swift, 2014). However, initiation into the parental way of life should at the same time ensure that children can relate to it reflectively in the long term. They must be involved discursively in significant life decisions, and they must be given opportunities to gain their own experiences with valuable social practices and projects in order to gradually understand themselves as agents with their own perspective (Betzler, 2011). This also requires that children get to know a variety of valuable options and ways of living. Defining the limits of legitimate parental authority in this way therefore does not rule out the possibility that children may one day reject their parents' views or retain them in a modified form by means of their own autonomous decision-making. For all the relevance ascribed to personal autonomy in the liberal-perfectionist conception advocated here, we do not agree with the strong focus of educational and political philosophy on the dangers of religious indoctrination, a focus also to be found in the public debate. This focus often operates with double standards, one that goes hand in hand with selective and therefore problematic attributions of heteronomy (especially in cases of religious, but not more or less secular forms of life) and that does not take sufficient account of other structural conditions that may undermine autonomy. These conditions involve, among others, the consequences of living in a capitalistically organized consumer culture (Schinkel et al., 2010).

Obliging parents to raise their children autonomously, and taking this obligation into account in the enactment of other childhood goods, does not necessarily amount to a systematic devaluation of traditional ways of life. It does, however, privilege autonomy-oriented forms of childrearing that amount to respecting children as persons and do not attempt to irreversibly commit children to a certain way of life. Only those educational practices are compatible with a good life for children that allow and encourage them to decide for themselves, sooner or later, how they want their life to go.

So much for the requirements of good parenting, which should also have made it clear that the well-known adage at the beginning of Tolstoy's Anna Karenina—"All happy families are alike; each unhappy family is unhappy in its own way"—is true only to a limited extent. There are many different and legitimate ways of realizing a good childhood in families and just as many ways of not fulfilling this parental responsibility. The goods of childhood not only provide sufficient scope for realizing a good childhood but also set limits that must be adhered to. Even if it is debatable in individual cases whether parents have adequately fulfilled this responsibility both from a moral and a legal standpoint, there are enough cases where these issues are largely clear-cut. After all, hardly anyone would seriously question that parents who do not provide their children with the material goods, relational goods, educational goods, or intrinsic childhood goods we have named are not sufficiently good parents. An upbringing that does not involve one or more childhood goods is—we should all agree—dysfunctional. The question of a good childhood in families is therefore not a completely 'open question.' An attempted escape into skirting our responsibilities as parents is therefore neither theoretically nor practically appropriate.

References

Badinter, E. (1991). *Die Mutterliebe: Geschichte eines Gefühls vom 17. Jahrhundert bis heute* (4th ed.). dtv.

Betzler, M. (2011). Erziehung zur Autonomie als Elternpflicht. *Deutsche Zeitschrift für Philosophie, 59*(6), 937–953.

Brighouse, H., & Swift, A. (2014). *Family values.* Princeton University Press.

Dornes, M. (2012). *Die Modernisierung der Seele: Kind—Familie—Gesellschaft.* Fischer.

El Mafaalani, A. (2021). *Mythos Bildung.* Kiepenheuer & Witsch.

Euteneuer, M., & Uhlendorff, U. (2020). *Familie und Bildungsalltag als Bildungsherausforderung.* Beltz.

Gheaus, A. (2018). What abolishing the family would not do. *Critical Review of International Social and Political Philosophy, 21*(3), 284–300.

Giesinger, J. (2015). Elterliche Rechte und Pflichten. In M. Betzler & B. Bleisch (Eds.), *Familiäre Pflichten* (pp. 107–127). Suhrkamp.

Lewis, S. (2023). *Die Familie abschaffen.* Fischer.

Mitterauer, M. (1991). Der Mythos von der vorindustriellen Großfamilie. In M. Mitterauer & R. Sieder (Eds.), *Vom Patriarchat zur Partnerschaft* (pp. 46–71). C.H. Beck.

Mitterauer, M., & Sieder, R. (1991). *Vom Patriarchat zur Partnerschaft.* C.H. Beck.

Schinkel, A., de Ruyter, D. & Steutel, J. (2010). Threats to Autonomy in Consumer Societies and Their Implications for Education, *Theory and Research in Education* 8, pp. 269–287.

Vaskovics, L. (2020). Soziale Elternschaft. *Zeitschrift für Erziehungswissenschaft, 23*(2), 269–293.
Winkler, M. (2012). *Erziehung in der Familie*. Kohlhammer.

CHAPTER 5

Childhoods in the Liberal State

Realizing a good childhood for all children is not the sole responsibility of parents; it is dependent upon a social infrastructure that should provide the institutional conditions to enact the goods of childhood to a sufficient extent. In line with the sufficiency-oriented position we advocate, social justice for children is a requirement that liberal states must guarantee. We are therefore not concerned with *equal opportunities* for children to have a good childhood, or that all childhoods should be *equally good*, but that they are *good enough*. Special attention is reserved for children whose situation—relative to the aforementioned minimum standard—is not only not good enough, but proves to be particularly bad. The complex relationship between the liberal state, parents, and children, which is sometimes referred to as the 'Bermuda triangle' of political theory, is the subject of ongoing controversy. One finds repeated debates about how the responsibilities, rights, and duties of all parties in the triangle should be balanced (such as debates about compulsory schooling or debates about the curricular canon). In the following, we argue that this relationship can be envisioned in the form of shared responsibility, whereby we are by no means committing ourselves to a model of harmony by means of a division of labor. On the contrary, any regulation of the relationship between parents, children, and the state is associated with moral and, of course, financial costs. If one holds on to the institution of the family—which we believe one should do from a liberal perspective in the absence of viable

J. Drerup, G. Schweiger, *What is a Good Childhood?*,
https://doi.org/10.1007/978-3-031-74237-8_5

alternatives—then compromises must be made in the realization of social justice.

The losses involved in such compromises cannot always be fully compensated for by state measures. Moreover, the goods of childhood as core elements of a good life for children cannot be justified neutrally in relation to all social groups and communities. Rather, they provide a suitable moral standard for evaluating the lives of *children as persons with their own moral status*. No variant of liberalism will accommodate all social interests and parental views in the same way, and each is associated with conflicts of connection. A liberal perfectionist view of a good childhood will generally resolve these conflicts so as to avoid any detriment of or disadvantages to children. This also seems to us to be the most suitable way of protecting children's legitimate interests in a sufficiently good childhood, even if it limits parents' ability to do what they want with their children at their own discretion. This stipulation does not necessarily amount to a direct restriction of parental rights and certainly does not support a political agenda of 'liberating' children from their parents but rather seeks to establish institutions that permanently improve children's chances of a good life. With regard to the distribution of responsibility for a good life, a distinction can be made between *primary* duties that different actors have directly toward children (e.g. in the family) and *secondary* duties that aim to ensure that these agents (are able to) fulfill these primary duties (Macleod, 2007). As we go through the various goods of childhood, we will see that in addition to its primary institutional, moral, and legal obligations, the liberal state has in many cases the additional role of ensuring, within the framework of secondary obligations toward children, that it is easier for families to fulfill their primary obligations. The task of the state in relation to parents is not so much to control parents but to support them in being good parents.

The state must provide social infrastructures that benefit everyone, especially vulnerable groups. These include children in poverty, underage refugees, children with serious chronic illnesses or disabilities, and all children who do not grow up in families but are dependent on public welfare institutions. External circumstances make it more difficult for these children to lead a good life, which is why they are dependent on additional help from state institutions. Trauma due to displacement, asylum-seeking, separation from the family, or growing up in a foreign country, for example, requires special psychological and therapeutic care from the state. We should provide this care so that these children can find their way in a new life and attain the core goods of childhood (Thiele, 2018).

We do not presuppose a naive-idealistic understanding of the liberal state but rather emphasize the necessity of criticizing the state's exploitation of children and childhood whenever it may occur (and there are plenty of historical and current examples of this). In doing so, we can then deconstruct various politically motivated ideals of childhood (Betz, 2022) and their normative assumptions regarding a good or a bad childhood. We need to examine such ideals for their blind spots and criticize them particularly when their supposedly child-friendly rhetoric actually conceals completely different social interests (such as economic or military interests). The five goods of childhood provide a normative framework for this critique.

One of the central problems in providing children with sufficient *material goods* is likely to be childhood poverty, which is almost always rooted in family poverty and which often affects single parents or immigrant families. Material provision and the socioeconomic status of the parents are important preconditions for almost all the goods of a good childhood. In order to successfully combat child poverty, a stable and sufficiently well-funded social welfare system is needed above all, one that compensates for material deficits in income, housing or food, and clothing. A basic child protection scheme that ensures that every child is provided for materially is one way of responding to this problem (Liebert, 2021). Modern societies are monetary societies, which means not only that (almost) all goods and services are purchased with money but also that money has an impact on all areas of social life. The lack of material goods has an impact on mental and physical health, one's self-understanding, and the educational opportunities open to the individual (Schweiger, 2022). This is just as true for children as it is for their parents. Under conditions of material deprivation, it is therefore also more difficult to achieve good parenting, that is, to provide children with sufficient material goods and the other goods of childhood. Material deprivation such as poverty, social exclusion, and unemployment create stress, anxiety, shame, and excessive demands upon families, which can have a negative impact on social relationships within and outside the family. It is therefore not surprising that violence and neglect are also more common under such conditions.

If it is the responsibility of the state to enable and protect justice for all children, that is, to ensure a good childhood for all children, then it must start with the social, health, and economic problems of the parents. Starting with the parents is crucial because parents are indispensable for a good childhood and the state is generally unable to compensate for a lack of good parenting. Since parents are so important for a good childhood, there are various options for how the state can intervene here. In extreme cases where children's rights are completely ignored, where parents do not fulfill fundamental duties, or commit obvious breaches of their children's well-being (such as physical violence, neglect, but also extreme forms of authoritarian parenting), the state is obliged to intervene.

In addition, consideration should be given to existing child and youth welfare services and the social infrastructure for poor families and children in general (Böllert, 2015). Here, increased education about the responsibilities of parenting in educational institutions and proposals for licensing parents could be considered (LaFollette, 2010). Proposals for licensing parenthood need not be so radical that the state massively interferes with people's rights to become parents by removing all children whose parents do not have a license from their families. The idea of licensing assumes that parents take on a great responsibility that obliges them to take good care of the child. The state requires this responsibility to be taken seriously, and it shows its commitment to children in providing various forms of support. For this reason, it seems sensible to implement licensing at least to the extent that the state creates sufficient low-threshold educational offers for (expectant) parents, advertises these accordingly, and ensures that it reaches all parents.

Relational goods are among the goods of childhood that cannot be distributed by the state. From the state's perspective, however, the social conditions for their enactment (especially with regard to parenthood) can be improved. Political policies involving children should serve to increase the likelihood that relational goods are sufficiently present in the lives of all children (e.g. through parental leave, reconciliation of family and work, improvement of the status of care work, and education). At the same time, relational goods are also supported to a significant extent in public educational institutions. These institutions can, among other things, help to ease the attachment of children to their parents, particularly where this attachment is detrimental to them, and they can at least partially compensate for such dysfunctional attachments. The almost-unshakeable loyalty that most children show to their parents, even if they are not sufficiently good parents and do not really deserve this loyalty, should give us pause for thought. Of course, the cultivation of relational goods in the form of care, affection, and friendships outside the family in educational and other institutions will only be able to compensate for this to a limited extent. However, this compensation, albeit limited, is all the more important so that children have the opportunity to develop alternative ideas of how the social world outside the family is shaped.

The central state authorities responsible for the enactment of *educational goods* are the preschool care system and the public school system. If schools can legitimately be expected to provide all students with a basic education in the form of basic cultural competencies, it must be noted that they do not meet this expectation for many students (in Germany, this holds for around a quarter of students after elementary school). In view of the enormous importance of basic education for the present and future of children, we believe it makes sense to speak of a right to education and a corresponding obligation on the part of the school system to fulfill this right. However, the sufficiency-oriented standard implied by this right does not settle all relevant debates about inequalities above and below the threshold. This is especially the case for the worst-off, who are confronted with the difficulties and challenges of life as functional illiterates. Unfortunately, the most diverse sector of the German and other educational systems—elementary school—where the most blatant educational inequalities could be tackled most effectively is chronically underfunded (El Mafaalani, 2021).

Education is not a panacea, and schools cannot solve every social problem that plagues our societies. But they must solve the task of providing basic education. Modern childhoods are childhoods that largely take place in schools. Learning does not always have to be fun and enjoyable, but the time and effort spent in school should be proportionate to the return. Proposals to de-school society are unlikely to improve the situation, particularly for the worst-off, but we can still ask the question of the kind of school that will actually prove to be *good* for children and not just a place where children waste their time. Here 'good' means simply capable of guaranteeing this basic prerequisite of a good childhood for all children. However one might describe this problem in detail, it seems too simplistic, in some cases downright absurd, to focus on just one single factor for educational reforms (such as the calls for more 'recognition of children' in schools) or even just to focus on schools to accomplish these reforms (and not also on the family and social environment). Where children can hope for little or no support from their parents, we believe it necessary to counteract the negative influence of one's socioeconomic background and to further expand the extracurricular care system for children and young people. As Axel Honneth puts it:

> The more stable, affectively reliable and close-knit such a childcare system would be—which would begin at the end of the first year of life and … support parental care, not replace it—the more that burdensome responsibility would fall away from the parents on the one hand and the more independent children would be from their parents' capacities to fulfill their duties on the other. (2015, p. 165)

In the concrete, we should support "increasing the quantity of places in publicly funded daycare facilities," improving the "quality of non-institutional daycare services" (Butterwegge & Butterwegge, 2021, pp. 261–263), improved forms of high-quality after-school programs, and the increased usage of multiprofessional teams in schools. The latter would help schools address the various educational and life problems of disadvantaged children. We considered it essential to promote such services, since they provide children with early opportunities for social integration and learning outside of school and home (Honneth, 2015, pp. 169–170).

The programs just named are also likely to be the places of education, play, and personal expression where children can be given state-funded access to the *intrinsic goods of childhood*. As with the other educational goods, the opportunities to enact these goods are distributed differently, and schools also have their contribution to make. Schools are neither mere repositories for children nor can their function be reduced solely to preparation for later life. The intrinsic goods of childhood are in danger of being neglected by the strong focus on the future-oriented functions and tasks of schools—particularly, in the now dominant rhetoric of competencies and learning outcomes. School learning, at least in the best cases, affects the current well-being and quality of children's lives.

Autonomy as a meta-good of a good childhood is a central point of contention in determining the relationship of authority and responsibility between parents and the state. Debates continually revolve around issues such as sex education and religious education. We as a public ceaselessly argue about compulsory schooling and exemptions for children of parents from religious communities. There is no need to overdramatize these conflicts. Generally, they are further outgrowths of the culture wars waged at the societal level, which often have little or nothing to do with children and their interests. Nevertheless, if we want to determine the necessary tasks of an autonomy-promoting education in state institutions, especially schools, clear guidelines should be set and boundaries drawn between state and parental education.

Above all, it is important that an *ethos of discontinuity* (Brighouse, 2007) prevails between home, society, and school, an ethos which should be oriented toward the meta-good of personal autonomy. This means that the rules for imparting knowledge and cultivating an understanding of the self and the world should be enacted in schools in relative independence from family and social influences. Not everything that is passed on in the family or society is worth bringing into schools. The rights of parents to influence the upbringing and education of their children at school are clearly limited here. Schools are places of education that are committed to the fundamental values of liberal democracy and the imparting of academic knowledge (Drerup, 2021). Parents may have a legal right to pass on their conception of the good to their children, but they have neither a legal nor a moral right to shield them from other views and bodies of knowledge or to withhold these from them. Their children are not their property to dispose of freely, nor are they entitled to colonize their future irreversibly in the name of their pet dogma. Children have a right to be given the opportunity to learn about alternatives to the views and values they have been taught at home. In this way, they can learn to ask questions without being anchored to a specific doctrine in advance. Gradually developing the practice of critical self-reflection and experiencing oneself as an independent individual is a core component of a good childhood. This practice should be promoted through an autonomy-promoting public educational system by the liberal state, whose legitimacy is also dependent on the autonomous consent of its citizens.

So much for the institutional conditions for the enactment of the goods of childhood that liberal states have to guarantee. Even though we have focused here on the state and the family, we believe that ensuring a good childhood is a task for society as a whole and that the associated responsibilities and costs should be borne by society as a whole. Ultimately, this means that everyone who deals with children in their everyday lives ought to contribute to this project—even if only in a very small way.

References

Betz, T. (2022). Leitbilder "guter Kindheit". Retrieved May 23, 2023, from https://www.bpb.de/shop/zeitschriften/apuz/kinder-und-politik-2022/506635/leitbilder-guter-kindheit/

Böllert, K. (2015). Familienformen im sozialen Wandel—Pluralität von Familienleitbildern in der Kinder- und Jugendhilfe? *Soziale Passagen, 7*, 191–204.

Brighouse, H. (2007). Channel One, the Anti-Commercial Principle, and the Discontinuous Ethos. In R. Curren (Ed.), *Philosophy of Education. An Anthology* (pp. 208–220). Blackwell.

Butterwegge, C., & Butterwegge, C. (2021). *Kinder der Ungleichheit: Wie sich die Gesellschaft ihrer Zukunft beraubt.* Campus Verlag.

Drerup, J. (2021). *Kontroverse Themen im Unterricht: Konstruktiv streiten lernen.* Reclam.

El Mafaalani, A. (2021). *Mythos Bildung.* Kiepenheuer & Witsch.

Honneth, A. (2015). Kindheit: Unstimmigkeiten unserer liberalen Vorstellungswelt. In M. Betzler & B. Bleisch (Eds.), *Familiäre Pflichten* (pp. 147–174). Suhrkamp.

LaFollette, H. (2010). Licensing parents revisited. *Journal of Applied Philosophy, 27*(4), 327–343.

Liebert, J. (2021). Vom Sinn der Kindergrundsicherung: Ein Vergleich grundlegender Reformkonzepte der Kinder und Familienförderung. *Sozial Extra, 45*(1), 24–30.

Macleod, C. (2007). Raising Children: Who is repsonsible for what?. In: Noggle, R. & Brennan, S. (Eds.), *Taking Responsibility for Children* (pp. 1–18). Wilfrid Laurier University Press.

Schweiger, G. (2022). *#Kinderarmut: Ein philosophischer Essay.* Büchner Verlag.

Thiele, H. (2018). Kindeswohl und Flucht: Minderjährige Geflüchtete als vulnerable Gruppe. In N. Pravan (Ed.), *Soziale Arbeit mit Geflüchteten: Rassismuskritisch, professionell, menschenrechtsorientiert* (pp. 118–133). Barbara Budrich.

CHAPTER 6

Conclusion and Outlook

In this book, we have put forward a view of the goods involved in a good childhood and discussed how the family and state might share responsibility in enacting these goods. In principle, the concept of a good childhood presented here provides a general framework that makes it possible to discuss questions of a good childhood in an ethically grounded and democratically legitimate way. Our view is, of course, still in need of further specification and interpretation, and it must be supplemented by additional empirical research. It is therefore also open to criticism and suggestions for improvement. Ultimately, readers must decide for themselves whether they believe it is plausible to interpret the life and moral status of children in this way.

The question of a good childhood always raises questions about our ethical and political self-understanding. How do we want to live together with children in the context of family, state, and society? What do we owe them as children and as growing individuals? In dealing with these questions, it is important to remain open-minded, particularly in our dealings with children and their perspectives. We can do this by constantly questioning whether a given understanding of childhood is ethically legitimate and pedagogically appropriate. Even if we assume that the enactment of the five goods of childhood will lead to moral progress for all children, we must nevertheless constantly remind ourselves of the temporality and mutability of our views on children. In earlier centuries or even just

J. Drerup, G. Schweiger, *What is a Good Childhood?*,
https://doi.org/10.1007/978-3-031-74237-8_6

decades, it was generally hard to imagine that children could be treated differently than they were—just think of the long struggle to abolish corporal punishment in schools, a struggle finally won not so long ago.

In closing, we would like to briefly discuss which strategies are best suited to improving the situation of children in light of our framework of childhood goods. We do not want to commit ourselves to a single approach, but assume that a combination of four different strategies is likely to be useful.

A *first* obvious and much-discussed approach is to *codify our aspirations for the treatment of children legally*. The idea is that by codifying children's rights transnationally and nationally and then implementing these legal requirements, we can best ensure that all children have a good childhood. This is supported by the fact that the law—at least in non-dysfunctional constitutional states—is probably one of the most efficient mechanisms for ensuring that moral standards are actually attained. There is indeed some evidence that this is the case, and stronger initiatives with regard to certain childhood goods would be highly desirable (cf. debates on the right to education, for example). Furthermore, it can be seen as a moral advance that children have constitutionally guaranteed rights to many of the goods of childhood in many countries. Nevertheless, children's rights are also highly open to interpretation and their codification does not guarantee implementation. Moreover, such implementation itself can often have paradoxical or unintended side effects that are not necessarily conducive to a good childhood in every case (e.g. in family law: Sutterly, 2017). Although legislation can itself trigger a change in social norms in favor of children, it does not necessarily do so (which is why it remains controversial whether, for example, children's rights in German Constitutional Law would have desired effects and not merely symbolic status). Furthermore, a certain inflation of rights can be observed today, particularly in the philosophical debate on children. It seems that there is now hardly anything that one does not have a right to. This rights inflation can lead to a devaluation of the language and normative currency of children's rights. There are some areas of life and some practices affecting children that cannot be fully legalized. Nor is it always clear why it should be plausible to assume that an ever-increasing expansion of children's rights is actually in the interests of children. The problems associated with achieving a good life for children cannot always be solved in the name of children's rights (Ben-Porath, 2020). This is especially true when such demands are combined with expansive political agendas for the liberation of children, which in our view often amounts to a mere 'letting loose' of children. Codifying and then implementing children's rights is therefore only *one* important strategy for improving the situation of children. The ethical, political, and educational debate should therefore not be limited to rights alone. Doing so prevents us from bringing several other important aspects of childhood into focus and recognizing some of the core elements of a good childhood.

A *second* strategy is to *improve existing educational institutions and social conditions of childrearing*. Despite all the legitimate criticism and need for improvement that undoubtedly exists here, it is important to recognize the complex, historically grown pedagogical rationality present in the school system and other child-related institutions (e.g. kindergartens and other extracurricular institutions). It seems highly unplausible to us to reject or abolish this rationality *in toto*. Of course, we can and should discuss what might be done better or differently. Proponents of radical and revolutionary reforms who claim to know how things could be done better in the name of a good childhood, or who simply claim that everything would miraculously get better if existing institutions were abolished, must therefore provide concrete and comprehensible reasons as to how exactly these reforms should look like in practice, what should replace the status quo, and why we should assume that the reformed state would actually be better for children's lives. Overly generalized critiques of schooling or the critique of generational orders alone are not enough. This is also one of the reasons why we have avoided referring to generalized and often overly pessimistic critical diagnoses of the situation of children and childhood in the modern world, diagnoses which usually have a very short half-life. Those who partake in such analyses regularly call for ambitious social-theoretical reframings of the discussion about childhood, usually without, however, providing these themselves or offering much in the way of ideas for improvement. Moreover, their claims are often made without sufficient empirical support or are patently false, since they tend to be based on symptomatic misconceptions that generalize individual cases (Dornes, 2012). And in the last analysis, they are almost always founded on normative assumptions about a good or a bad childhood that they do not systematically explicate or even recognize themselves.

A *third* strategy is to *take children more seriously* as *political agents and enable them to participate in the democratic process*. There are many ways to implement this strategy. In our view, there is little reason not to cultivate democratic practices in families and schools and also to discuss new regulations on the legal voting age (Giesinger, 2022). When doing so, we should keep in mind that we are dealing with children—democratic participation in education and politics will always be structurally asymmetric and therefore cannot be comprehensively democratized. Furthermore, the ideal of a well-informed and permanently engaged citizen, which is often assumed in such views, is probably only met by a negligible proportion of the adult population. Adopting such an ideal for children is therefore misguided. More participation is not always better. Children's political participation is often associated with overly high hopes, which in many cases turn out to be projections by adults who no longer trust themselves to shape the social world politically. Such a delegation of responsibility is questionable at best. It even suggests that there may be something to contemporary critiques of widespread infantilization that claim that many adults—deep down—do not want to be adults at all. Even if this does not rule out the increased involvement of children in democratic decision-making processes, it is primarily adults who have a duty to take responsibility for decisions in the family and society, decisions that are ultimately conducive to achieving a good childhood for all.

A *fourth* strategy is to raise awareness of and publicly address issues relating to children and childhood, a strategy we hope to have advanced with this book. From a historical perspective, a welcome change in social norms can be recognized in this domain. Today, there is a broader social awareness of the situation and interests of children. The impetus for developing alternative forms of coexistence with children has repeatedly come from initiatives in civil society, whose proposals have given rise to critical public debate on various relevant issues. The increased, albeit belated, public attention to children in the context of the corona pandemic can certainly give hope here (Drerup, 2022).

Experience has shown that, while strides may be made in the *pedagogical implementation* of these four strategies (as much educational optimism is allowed), their *political implementation* is generally the sticking point. With the questions and problems of childhood, the closer you get to them politically, the bigger they become. That is, the more we focus our attention on them, the more dilemmas arise, the greater the empirical imponderables seem, and the more political conflicts of interest loom on the horizon. It is almost as if the more we offer models and strategies for shaping childhood, the more difficult it becomes not only to justify decisions but also to implement them. Nevertheless, despite all the difficulties, we believe it is possible to achieve a good childhood for all children (or at least to come closer to this goal). The conception of childhood presented in this book should not be regarded as utopian, but as hopeful—hopeful that, in light of the concrete aspects of a good childhood we have outlined, we can now, as a society, get to work. After all, our children may one day ask us why we have left them the flawed world they now have to navigate, and why we did not do what we could have done to make it better.

References

Ben-Porath, S. (2020). *Tough choices. Structured paternalism and the landscape of choice*. Princeton University Press.

Dornes, M. (2012). *Die Modernisierung der Seele: Kind—Familie—Gesellschaft*. Fischer.

Drerup, J. (2022). *Kinder, Corona und die Folgen*. Campus.

Giesinger, J. (2022). *Wahlrecht—auch für Kinder?* Metzler.

Sutterly, F. (2017). Normative Paradoxien der rechtsstaatlichen Sorge um das Kindeswohl. In F. Sutterly & D. Flick (Eds.), *Der Streit um das Kindeswohl* (pp. 52–88). Beltz.

Index[1]

[1] Note: Page numbers followed by 'n' refer to notes.

J. Drerup, G. Schweiger, *What is a Good Childhood?*,
https://doi.org/10.1007/978-3-031-74237-8

Printed by Printforce, the Netherlands